Follow Me
DISCIPLESHIP THAT MOVES US

Brian Kannel

Published by CCS Publishing
23890 Brittlebush Circle
Moreno Valley, CA 92557 USA
1-888-344-CELL

ISBN: 978-1-935789-44-4

CCS Publishing is the book-publishing division of Joel Comiskey Group, a resource and coaching ministry dedicated to equipping leaders for cell-based ministry.

Find us on the World Wide Web at www.joelcomiskeygroup.com

Contents

Introduction

In April of 2010, God used the Eastern Pennsylvania District Superintendent and the Elders of York Alliance to call me into the role of Lead Pastor of York Alliance Church (YAC). I must say, that mantle was one I accepted with more than a little hesitation, fear, and trepidation! Much of that was related to the heavy weight of responsibility that comes from such a position along with my continued realization that I am fallen, broken, and incapable of adequately filling such a role in my own strength. However, through nearly a year of deeply hearing from God, I had become convinced that He was leading me into this role, and that His strength would be made perfect in my weakness.

The church that I inherited had many incredible strengths. Among them was a clearly defined vision statement that neither I nor the leadership had any intention or desire to change. It reads as follows:

> York Alliance Church is seeking to be an outreach-based church, committed to exalting Christ and loving people by becoming disciples that make disciples. In all of this, prayer is the first work.

In some ways, this statement had provided the filter that was necessary for us to embrace over the past 15 years of ministry. However, as I evaluated our church, the spiritual growth of our congregation, the development of the dozens and dozens who had come to faith over the past several years of ministry, and the issues that had been challenging and even divisive during those same years, I realized that there were two questions that needed to be answered.

The first question was this: What are the core values that make York Alliance the church that it is, and more importantly, the church we long to be? There are many churches that would affirm our vision statement, but that choose to do ministry in very different ways than we did it. While we were in no way opposed to various ways of doing ministry, it was vital for us to understand what we would be about, and stick to those ways. Through much study, discussion, and prayer, we arrived at seven "Family Values," which make up the subject matter of this book. The determination of these seven values was absolutely vital to who we are as a church, and they soon became a much better filter for ministry than our vision statement had provided.

The second question proved to be a more difficult one: What is the basic process for discipleship at York Alliance Church? We were not a church cluttered by programs—we had transitioned to a cell church model a decade earlier and had eliminated just about all extraneous programs in that transition. However, as I wrestled with this question personally and asked the same question of dozens of key leaders, our responses were mostly blank stares. Sure, there were paths in which a person might become a disciple. We had acquired a series of books that provided a path for discipleship, even though very few actually utilized them. Several mentoring/discipling relationships were working well in the 1:1 setting. The "right" LIFE group (our name for our cell groups) could effectively provide a path for some who were wired in the right ways. However, we all agreed: There simply was not a clear, identifiable, and easily communicated path for growth in the faith.

And so we wrestled—for months. We talked through what was necessary for growth. We talked about our newly minted values and how they related to our vision. We talked about images that brought visual clarity to theoretical concepts and processes. And ultimately, we arrived at a process. A relatively simple one, and, hopefully, a clear one. If the Family Values make up the subject matter of this book, it's the hourglass discipleship model that gives it structure and form and, I pray, that brings these theoretical concepts into practical, everyday life… because, values that don't get dirty in the dust and grime of everyday life aren't worth all that much, no matter how true they are.

That's the context for all that follows. When Jesus called His disciples at the beginning of His ministry, He did so with a simple command: "Follow Me." The incredible truth that we so often miss is that the New Testament writers assumed that, as we grow in our faith, we would indeed actually become more and more like Him. This is nowhere more evident than in Jesus' own teachings. Yet, so few in the church actually reflect this truth. May we, dear reader, by the grace of Jesus, be those who do.

Here's to the journey.

Grace and peace,

Brian Kannel
York Alliance Church

CHAPTER ONE
Vision, Values and Process

"There is a great market for religious experience in our world; there is little enthusiasm for the patient acquisition of virtue, little inclination to sign up for a long apprenticeship in what earlier generations of Christians called holiness."
– Eugene Peterson

If you know me, or if you've every taken a quick glance at a photo of me, you'll recognize that I'm follically challenged. Bald would be more direct... and no, I won't be offended if you call me that! The fact is, I've been this way for just about all of my adult life. For years, I've blamed my high school theatre director, Louie Mattachione, who made me shave my head every day for a month in order for it to "shine" as I played Daddy Warbucks in my senior musical. After that traumatic experience, my thick head of hair wasn't quite so... thick. However, the reality is that it was going to happen anyway. Anyone who got a C or better in high school genetics knows that male baldness comes directly from the grandfather on the mother's side, and my Grandpa George's early pictures confirmed my worst fears: clear male-pattern baldness by the time he could vote. I was doomed from the beginning. It was in the DNA.

Vision and DNA
Every church has its own DNA. It's a statement that I believe with all my heart. Vision has the luxury of being rather general, particularly within the

high level mission and vision statements that are seen throughout Western churches. At York Alliance, we state our vision this way:

> *York Alliance Church is seeking to be an outreach-based church, committed to exalting Christ and loving people by becoming disciples that make disciples. In all of this, prayer is the first work.*

And that's good... at least as vision statements go. But honestly, what self-respecting church *wouldn't* affirm that? Of course, every church might use different words and phrases to communicate it, but the heart would remain. Name a church that is boldly declaring:

> *"We exist completely for ourselves, and could honestly not care less about the world around us. Jesus is great and all, but worship is a bit overrated. We like some people, but loving all people is really asking too much. Discipleship? Way too hard. In fact, the only thing harder is making other disciples. Forget that stuff—we're about complacency and comfort. See that? Alliteration. We must be on the right track. Oh, and prayer? For us, we'd like to keep it purely ceremonial. Honestly, we don't believe there's any real power in it, but saying a prayer now and then sure provides a good opening or closing to meetings, and it's a great way to transition between songs. Any questions?"*

I'm not saying there aren't many churches, present company included, that don't *act* at times as though these things are true. It would be foolish to say that any church made up of broken people in a broken world might not, at least now and then, fall into these pitfalls. However, no church is printing up stationary with that statement printed in script along the bottom. No one's aiming for the high goal of lukewarm acknowledgement and comfort, with a few sides of ceremonial tradition and self-focus thrown in. Vision, at least as contained in a statement like ours, is basically what it means to be the Church. In that way, vision acts more like a species identification tool, stating in no uncertain terms what qualities are necessary in order to even be called a "church" biblically.

Values and DNA

DNA, however, is completely different. I remember learning about those magical spirals in middle school, and how fascinating it was that those tiny pieces of matter contained the blueprint for every variation of who we are compared to everyone else. The factors that DNA addresses aren't so much the things that make us "human" as opposed to some other species. Rather, they address the variety of human that we will be. Despite many evil and destructive ideas throughout generations, there isn't something inherently better or worse about eye color, skin color, or hair color. Tall or short, skinny or ... not; big feet or small feet or even different-sized feet[1]—these are not factors of "better or worse" but ones that are simply "different". The "better or worse" valuation is based only on function. For instance, if I need to reach something on a high shelf, "tall" might be preferable. However, if I need to squeeze into a small opening, or a Mini Cooper, "short" would be a better choice. One trait isn't inherently better than the other, but one might be better suited for a specific task.

Church DNA functions identically. There are churches that are easily identified by things like: worship style, denominational affiliation, the appearance (or lack of appearance) or certain spiritual gifts, tightly held theological stances, specific ministry styles, type of preaching, community involvement, building décor and style, focus on a specific generation, affinity for bad coffee and potluck dinners... and the list could go on and on. Each of these, and lots of others, have their place in the culture of Christendom. Preference of one over the other is simply that—preference. However, every local church also exists within a culture: neighborhoods, people from various backgrounds, educational histories and church-experience (or lack of it), technological factors, pop culture influences, etc. Due to these factors, churches with a variety of DNA are often necessary to effectively minister to the diverse cultures around them, and churches with certain DNA might be better-suited to address the specific needs of a

---

1 Yes, my right foot is a size 13 and my left is a size 11. I maintain, with such perfection in every other way, spare parts were needed for my feet. Or something like that...

specific community, much like a tall person is better suited to get the can of kidney beans off the top shelf.

The question, then, that every church must ask is this: "What is our DNA?" In other words, who are we called, even destined, to be that is uniquely us? Without a clear determination of these factors, the DNA of the church will become the DNA of a handful of strong personalities in the church body, whether that is best for the church as a whole or not. At York Alliance, the DNA quest led our leadership team to realize that our vision statement, while effective and biblical, simply acted to distinguish our species (*churchus americanus* is, I think, the correct species name), not our unique DNA.

What made us unique as a church? We determined seven factors, or *values*, that rested comfortably underneath the umbrella of our vision statement, and which stated who we currently are as well as who we hoped to be. Over time, these became known as our "Family Values" which we state in this way:

Prayer as the First Work

We believe prayer is literally the very first and most important work that we are called to as believers. This is a forthright acknowledgment that all transformation, all real heart movement, any impact on people or systems—anything that truly lasts—is the work of God and not the work of man. We will always seek to operate in dependence on the Holy Spirit in all things, seeking His work among us and joining Him in it, not running ahead or lagging behind. The real work of the church is work that only God can do.

The Foundation of the Word

We believe that God has revealed Himself in His Word, the Bible, and that His Word is central and foundational to all of life. Inherent in this truth is that the Bible is God's Word about Himself, according to His plan and His purpose. It's not a self-help book for my problems, a road map for my life, or a magic charm that blesses my every move. Rather, it's the revelation of the God of the Universe and His action in the world. When we are grounded in that understanding of the Word, we have a solid foundation.

Worship as a Lifestyle

We believe that beyond simply a celebration gathering, all of life is to be lived as an act of worship to God. Songs, Scripture declarations, giving, creedal affirmations and corporate prayer are expressions of worship, but never the totality of it. Worship is a willful and intentional connection of every aspect of my life to every aspect of God. Further, it's a representation of a life that readily declares the gospel in my everyday living and in my community. Worship is an offering of my life as a living sacrifice before God. With this understanding, we are to be worshipers.

Authentic Community

We believe that God has called us to live with one another in mind, being open and honest with other believers in our journey towards Christ. We recognize that when we fail to live authentically before one another, we lose the ability to genuinely give and receive love and, therefore, grow disconnected. Striving to be a place where it's "OK not to be OK," we will lovingly confront sin in order to see holiness emerge, tenderly nurture brokenness in order to see wholeness emerge, and gently acknowledge pain in order to see peace emerge. All of these must be handled through the lens of the Gospel of Jesus.

Serving the Body

We believe that God has given every believer in Jesus at least one gift that is to be used for the building up of the church and for the blessing of the world. The use of each of these gifts is necessary if the body of Christ is to grow to maturity. However, beyond the empowering and release of the gifts of the Spirit, there is simply a need to serve one another in basic ways within the body of Christ just as Jesus did. When He washed the disciples' feet, it wasn't because that was His spiritual gift or the best use of His time and energy—it was because He loved the Church. We must do the same.

Missional Living

We believe that God is in the process of reconciling the world to Himself through Jesus, and that we've been allowed a part in that process. Every aspect of our life is to be focused on the mission of becoming disciples who make other disciples, both in our local communities and to the ends of the earth. God in His sovereignty has established the times, positions, locations, and events of our daily living and has placed us within them in order to proclaim His truth. He has also entrusted us with the message of reconciliation for the lost world, and we must live sacrificially with that end in mind.

Shalom of the City

We believe that our lives need to be driven by the purpose for which God has created us: to glorify Him and to help others all around the world to do the same. As children of God, we own nothing but are stewards of everything. Therefore, all that we have is intended to bring peace and justice into the middle of the situations in which we find ourselves, and we are called to use the energies, passions, and resources that we've been given to work for the peace of our city.

While each of these values has a clear Biblical foundation (after all, that is, in itself, one of our values!), not every local church in the world would state these as *their* top priorities or primary characteristics. Like hair color, height, and the ability to curl one's tongue into a "U" shape, these are not intended to be factors for the value or effectiveness of any local church… except for ours. At York Alliance, we want to constantly evaluate these factors because, for us, they *are* a measure of effectiveness—whether or not we are becoming the church that God has called us to be. We want to teach these values regularly, insuring that all that call our church body their family will understand them well, in order for us to have consistent DNA as the local body of Christ. We want to display these values in increasing measure, through our outward and observable actions, both as individuals and as a corporate body. Just like a young woman who's naturally gifted to be a world-class poet, we don't want to squander our gifting by spending all of our time playing basketball with our friends and never reading great literature or trying our hand at writing a poem. While basketball is a wonderful activity for some, it's important that we remember who we're called to be and to not wander too far from it.

Of course, embracing these values doesn't discount the great variety of gifting and personality within our local body. These values, while quite specific in some ways, have an incredible variety of applications. Maintaining a lifestyle of worship has direct application to every area of our life, regardless of our specific personality and life calling. However, as a church, we want to constantly help one another make that specific application to our daily lives, not simply exist from Sunday to Sunday, or from LIFE group meeting to LIFE group meeting, without a thought of what it means to be a worshiper in each of our life settings. We want to maintain a great diversity of expression while simultaneously holding to a great unity of direction and value.

Process and DNA

So I'm bald—destined to be, based on genetic code. DNA, passed from grandfather to mother to me, has determined it. However, it didn't always look that way. I remember the barber marveling about how incredibly thick my hair was as a pre-teen and teenager. I remember the simultaneous cut and tear of the thinning shears as he tried, often with little success, to manage the thick mass of sometimes straight and sometimes wavy hair that sat on my head like a mop. The genetic reality is that *every factor that would contribute to my baldness was already present in my life*. However, I just didn't know it. Nor did my frustrated barber, who would have been much happier cutting my hair today (which, by the way, I do myself—it's not a difficult job!). DNA is constant in its presence, but it's often progressive in its expression. The same is true for both the local church and the individual believer in Jesus.

After the family values had been determined and affirmed, our leadership team set about answering the question: "What is the basic process for discipleship at this specific local church?" In other words, what is the process through which these DNA factors take root more deeply within us? We wrestled with the process itself as well as with a way to effectively communicate that process. How do we express something that is both constantly present but also infinitely progressive? How do we respond to values that co-exist, but also vary in the fullness of their expression at various times throughout a week, month, or year? What about factors that lead into one another, but also cycle around following one another? And most of all, how do we avoid the very common error that all of this somehow depends on *our* effort, not on the transformational grace of Jesus in our midst?

Following months of prayer, we stumbled upon the image of the hourglass. It was simultaneously static and progressive: the sand moved within the system, but never outside of the system. It was directional and cyclical at the same time: the sand moved from top to bottom, but once the path was completed, the hourglass was turned over, the bottom now becoming the top, and the process began all over again. It evoked both the temporal and the eternal at the same time: one "cycle" of the hourglass had a finite beginning and end, but the cycles could continue infinitely and, as long as the hourglass was "useful," they *would* continue. However, most importantly, every cycle had a crisis point: No grain of sand could pass from top to bottom without encountering the center of the hourglass.

So our discussion of discipleship started to sound something like this: There are environments in which we intentionally position ourselves in order for God to work in our lives. Some of these environments include corporate and personal worship, the intimate and intentional community of a LIFE group or mentoring relationship, and the study of God's Word. These environments are represented by the top half of the hourglass. Within these environments, we encounter the transformational power of

Jesus through the gospel[2], and, consequently, something new is generated within us. This could be a first time encounter with Jesus (conversion/salvation) or one of any number of encounters with Him subsequent to (or even prior to!) salvation. Regardless, something is generated in us within that encounter—new passion, a refreshed spirit, spiritual gifts, vision, energy, etc. The specifics of *what* is generated will be different every time, but the fact that *something* is generated is inherent within the encounter with Jesus[3]. This, of course, is represented by the center point of the hourglass. That which is generated, then, is not intended to terminate on us. The blessing of God, whatever the form, is intended to be poured out into the community and world around us, which is represented by

the bottom half of the hourglass. Our lives are poured out as the hands and feet of Jesus in the world around us, taking expression both inside and outside the body of Christ, both locally and globally, and in the form of everything from evangelism to ministry to the creation of art and culture. The common factor is that each of these expressions of lives poured out is focused on God being glorified. Once lives are poured out, whatever the form, the hourglass must be refreshed (turned back over), and we must intentionally place ourselves in the environment in which we can once again encounter the transforming work of Jesus. The general process is represented in Figure 1.1 to the right:

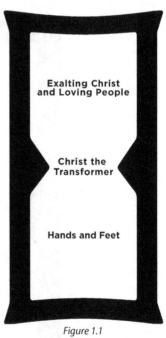

Exalting Christ and Loving People

Christ the Transformer

Hands and Feet

Figure 1.1

---

2 There is much good discussion happening currently about how "gospel" is best defined. However, that discussion is outside of the scope of this book. For our purposes, "gospel" will simply mean the atoning work of Jesus in His life, death, and resurrection, offering us new life through His Spirit.

3 This concept will be further developed within Chapter 5: Prayer, the First Work.

With this image in mind, it's not difficult to see how the Family Values fit in. Through the process represented by the hourglass, we can experience each of these values at every stage of our spiritual journey, from infancy to maturity, as they more deeply take root within us both individually and corporately. It also provides an evaluation tool whereby we can measure our strength or weakness in expressing the values: for instance, strong expression represented through the deep and intimate community, or weak expression represented through not being driven by the missional heart of Jesus in our everyday living. The cohesion, then of the Family Values with the hourglass process of discipleship would look like this:

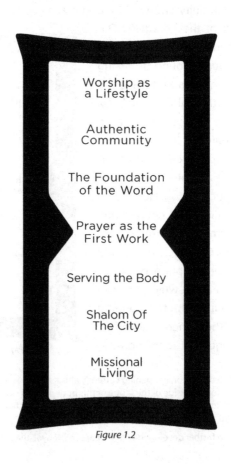

Figure 1.2

It's in this image that the heart of York Alliance Church can be seen, and I believe that heart of every individual's pursuit of Jesus. Our vision is to be outreach-based by exalting Christ and loving people, becoming and making disciples, being driven by the first work of prayer. Our values, then, flow out of that vision: We live as worshipers, connecting authentically in community, based firmly in the foundation of the Word of God. We are then transformed by the work of Jesus through prayer. It's this transformation that leads us to serve one another within the body of Christ, bring peace to the world through our presence in it, and have lives that are driven by the mission of Jesus to take His message into all of the world. Each of these values fit into a constantly moving, dynamic process that is changing us into the likeness of Jesus with ever increasing glory! (2 Corinthians 3:18)

Sound exciting? What we have found in our small community is that, through a commitment to these values and a resolve to rely on God's transforming power in our lives and not our own, we are constantly being changed. Of course, there are huge holes and deep brokenness. In fact, as we learn to be truly authentic with one another (see Chapter 3), the holes seem to be larger and more numerous than ever before. However, in the midst of that, we are seeing real transformation: lives saved by grace, marriages restored, people who have been broken, in part by the church itself, now healed and ministering effectively, and those who have been stagnant for years now alive and growing in new and incredible ways. How does this happen? Only by the grace of Jesus and His work. He is the One leading toward transformation, and we simply need to follow Him.

So, what do you say? Shall we begin? Just as a grain of sand finds itself at the top of the hourglass, we'll journey through, one value at a time.

Vision, Values and Process
Questions for Reflection

1. As you look at the seven values, which one resonates most with you? Which one resonates the least?

2. In your own journey of faith, do you feel like you tend to spend more time in the top or the bottom of the hourglass? Why do you think that is?

3. Does the hourglass image well describe your discipleship journey? Why or why not? Is there another image or metaphor you might use?

4. What makes you most excited about this journey? Is there anything that makes you apprehensive?

CHAPTER TWO
Lifestyle of Worship

"If we will not worship God seven days a week, we do not worship Him one day a week. There is no such thing known in heaven as Sunday worship unless it is accompanied by Monday worship and Tuesday worship and so on…"
- A.W. Tozer

One of the most well-known missionaries of the 20th century was a man named Eric Liddell. His story, made famous in the movie <u>Chariots of Fire</u>, revolved around two seemingly opposite passions: the gospel of Jesus and running. Liddell was driven by his passion for Jesus into mainland China during a very difficult and dangerous time in the first half of the 20th century, spending long periods of time separated from his wife and daughters due to the extreme danger of the areas in which he was serving. However, it was his passion for running that drove him to compete for gold in the 1924 Paris Olympics.

Liddell was a sprinter, and his best event was the 100 meters, in which he was among the best in the world. Leading up to the Paris games, the track and field schedule was published, along with the heat schedules for the 100 meters—with a qualifying heat scheduled on Sunday. Liddell, in honor of the Sabbath, had always refused to compete on Sundays. It seemed that his two passions were headed for a collision course. However, there was no real conflict, at least in Liddell's heart and mind. Once the schedule was published and he saw the conflict, he withdrew from the 100 meters and began to train for the 200 meters instead. Despite it not being his best event, Liddell won the gold in Paris before returning to the field in China where he faithfully proclaimed the gospel of Jesus and served refugees, prisoners, and the poor.

What is worship? A hymn sung on a Sunday morning? Bowing down before a god and uttering some prayers before moving on with life? Is it simply a genre of music in the local Christian bookstore? Or could it be that worship is far more than that? Liddell famously said it this way: "I believe God made me for a purpose, but He also made me fast. And when I run, I feel His pleasure." Worship, indeed.

Troubling Statistics

In a 2009 CNN poll, 75% of Americans described themselves as Christian.[4] The easy thing, of course, is to put imaginary finger quotes around "Christian" in your mind and to marginalize that number. In many ways, of course, that's justified. We live in a country where "Christian" is often viewed more as a cultural, almost ethnic, distinction than it is a statement of faith or belief. There are many who proudly wear the label "Christian" and yet deny many basic precepts that define the term itself: the deity of Jesus, the exclusivity of His claims, the incarnation, the atoning death of Jesus on the cross for our sins, the bodily resurrection, etc. So maybe that number, 75%, doesn't mean much to you. How about this one:

According to the Pew Forum, 26% of Americans are Evangelical.[5] At least that's the way they would describe themselves. So what does evangelical mean? Barna defines evangelicals as those who

> *"...have made a personal commitment to Jesus Christ that is still important in their life today and who also indicate they believe that when they die they will go to Heaven because they have confessed*

---

4 March 9th, 2009 article, "America becoming less Christian, survey finds" on cnn.com/living

5 According to www.religions.pewforum.org, as of April 11th, 2012

their sins and accepted Jesus Christ as their Savior. They say their faith is very important in their life today; they believe that they have a personal responsibility to share their religious beliefs about Christ with non-Christians; they believe that Satan exists; they believe that eternal salvation is possible only through grace, not works; they believe that Jesus Christ lived a sinless life on earth; they assert that the Bible is accurate in all that it teaches; and they describe God as the all-knowing, all-powerful, perfect deity who created the universe and still rules it today."[6]

26% of Americans believe that. 1 in 4. Every fourth person you meet, see, interact with, or pass on the road believes that. Actually, unless you're reading this from your Oregon home overlooking the Pacific or downtown Manhattan, the number is probably closer to 1 in 3.

Does that number bother you? If not, it may be because you're not seeing through the right lens. So let me ask the question another way: Does the world around us *look* like 25% of the people believe in, passionately pursue, trust and hope in the person of Jesus?

"Houston, we have a problem."

Defining the Problem
So what's the problem? There are those that would say that we have a doctrine problem: that the modern church has given in to the cultural pressures of relativism and postmodernism, and because we no longer hold the truth as tightly as we once did, the gospel message is watered down and emptied of its power. And honestly, I'm all for doctrine. In fact, full disclosure, I'm a bit of a theological fanatic. When I hear something, I tend to sift it through the filter of a biblical theology, which has resulted in some very interesting conversations with my children. This past December, my 10 year old daughter Tia and 3 year old son Micah were driving with me

---

6 "Survey Explores Who Qualifies as an Evangelical", www.barna.org, January 18th, 2007.

away from the mall about a week before Christmas. Out of nowhere, Micah makes a proclamation:

> **Micah:** *I know God and Jesus.*
> **Tia:** *That's good, buddy!*
> **Micah:** *(clearly not getting the hoped for reaction) I like God and Jesus!*
> **Me:** *(clearly being too much of a pastor) How about the Holy Spirit, buddy? Do you like the Holy Spirit too?*
> **Tia:** *Yeah, buddy, like the Trinity. God the Father, Jesus, and the Holy Spirit—they're three different people, but they're all one God! Isn't that cool? (clearly having already had one too many of these conversations with her father)*
> **Micah:** *(now yelling) NO! I like God, Jesus, and Santa Claus!*

Micah's version of the Trinity notwithstanding, doctrine has a vital place in the church. We need to be clear on issues like truth and life and morality, because God's greatest glory and our greatest joy have been revealed to us through the Word, and we should know what it says. However, I can't help but look at the early church and see the profound impact that they made on the world around them, even while Peter and Paul, its two most influential leaders, argued about something as basic as whether salvation was by grace alone or had a physical and cultural component as well. It seems that, while good doctrine is incredibly important, it's likely not the real problem.

There are others who argue that the problem is with our structure and programming. The challenge here is that there are incredible stories of success on every side of the argument! There are those who are driven by purpose, sensitive to seekers, building the believers, investing in small groups of every kind *(Do you have a small group for left-handed softball players? Of course! Mondays at 7:00 in the basement!)*, exploding with evangelism, stripping down the programs, multiplying (never dividing!) cells, making church simple, or deep, or sticky, or complete… and that barely scratches the surface. Here's the problem: there's a success story that goes with every one of these systems! If the system didn't work, at least in their setting, there wouldn't have been a publishing deal, and honestly, no one would care. However, if all different kinds of structures and programs, even ones that directly conflict with one another, have varying degrees of success, it seems that the problem is not primarily a structural one.

There are still others that argue the problem is a moral one. We, the church, have been drawn away by the world around us, no longer simply being "in it" but "of it" as well. And there's certainly no denying that very visible church leaders have been embroiled in very visible scandal again and again over the past decades. It seems there's always another survey revealing that factors such as pornography usage, alcoholism, sexual promiscuity, eating disorders, drug abuse, and divorce are just as pronounced (if not, at times, worse!) for those inside the church as with those outside of it. So is the problem a moral one? Do we simply need to try harder to be better people so that we can make a real impact on the world?

Church history acts as the teacher in this instance. While there are certainly deplorable moral situations within the church today, this is in no way a unique situation. The church over the centuries has been built on the back of sexual addicts (Augustine), slave traders (John Newton), anti-Semites (Martin Luther), those who were often depressed to the point of suicide (Charles Spurgeon), and many other unsavory characters. Maybe the clearest example is King David, the man whom God Himself declared was one after His own heart, who committed adultery with the wife of a close friend, and then had him murdered so he wouldn't be found out. While our lives must be a part of the testimony that we speak to the world, and, therefore, should line up with God's best for us, it seems that morality isn't the primary reason for the ineffectiveness of the church.

So what is the problem? Could it be that our primary problem is really a *worship* problem? Our lives are so often lived in such a way that relegates worship to a daily or weekly activity and, in doing so, we miss the message of Liddell's beautiful declaration: "When I *run*, I feel His pleasure." Do we feel His pleasure when we cook and clean? When we are closing business deals? When we are leading our classrooms or designing lesson plans? When we are working the line at the factory or closing up the patient in the operating room? How about when we serve our spouses, care for our kids, love our neighbors, and bear the light of Jesus into the dark world around us? Are any of these things intended to be *less* worshipful than singing at the top of our lungs, eyes closed and hands raised, on a Sunday morning?

Living Sacrifices
In his letter to Roman Christians, the apostle Paul gives us a very broad and inclusive definition of worship. He says it this way: *"I appeal to you therefore, brothers, by the mercies of God, to present your bodies as a living sacrifice, holy and acceptable to God, which is your spiritual worship." (Romans 12:1)* There are a few vital pieces of this definition that we need to see clearly if we are to live lives of worship.

"…by the mercies of God." The mercy of Jesus toward us always precedes our worship. His mercy is never earned, qualified for, purchased, or conned by our worship. This is the great distinction of the Christian faith, one that mustn't be lost in the cultural milieu. Every other faith or religious philosophy operates in the completely opposite order: you serve, you worship, you give, you sacrifice, and then *and only then* is the mercy of god (or karma or life force) given to you. However, Christianity says just the opposite: *"This is love, not that we have loved God but that he loves us and sent his Son to be the propitiation (the one who bore the wrath of God in our place) for our sins." (1 John 4:10, definition added)* We don't earn mercy, but we respond to God out of the mercy that He's already given freely to us in Jesus.

"…present your bodies." What is our response to the overwhelming mercy of God shown at the cross? We "present" our bodies, or dedicate ourselves, to Him out of thankfulness and praise. The word translated "present" (ESV) or "offer" (NIV) is really a ceremonial term for bringing a sacrifice as an offering of worship. The sense is that this object or being is fully dedicated

to the act of worship—100% devoted to that act. The distinction can be lightheartedly seen in the mythical discussion between the pig and the chicken as they walk down the road. They see a homeless man and, taking pity on him, the chicken suggests that they make him a nice ham and egg breakfast. The pig says to the chicken: "Easy for you to say! For you that requires an offering—but for me, it's a total sacrifice!" The story is a corny one, but the idea holds up: What am I fully devoted to? What is the primary focus of my thoughts? My resources? My time? My passion? What activity, when it's disturbed, makes me angry? Chances are, those are the things to which I am dedicated. Paul says that, in response to the mercy of God, we should be dedicated to Him alone.

"…as a living sacrifice." The things to which I'm dedicated are things for which I will also sacrifice. Money spent on a favorite hobby, time spent with close friends, inconvenience experienced for the sake of my children or my family—these are sacrifices joyfully made for the sake of that to which I'm dedicated. A simple formula might look like this:

Dedication + Sacrifice = Worship

Under this definition, worship cannot be simply seen as a church or religious activity! Rather, anything that I'm dedicated to and will sacrifice for becomes an object of worship to some degree. Of course, there are constantly areas of life that require a modicum of dedication and some level of sacrifice—job, family, home ownership, friendship, education and good health all immediately come to mind. However, in reference to the pig and chicken, there is a difference between an *offering* and a *total sacrifice*. Liddell was certainly dedicated and made a long series of sacrifices to become one of the best sprinters in the world during the summer of 1924. Yet, when faced with the call to sacrifice one area of dedication for a greater one, the choice was immediate. However, when I'm *not* faced with such a radical choice, how can I tell whether I'm doing an activity to the glory of God or making that activity *into* a god? Paul will answer that question for us in his next sentence.

The Transformation Test

Worship is not an activity I do in order to earn favor and mercy from God, but rather is a response to the favor and mercy God has already shown me. Dedication and sacrifice are the dual aspects that combine to equal worship in the broad sense. Therefore, when I am dedicated to something and willing to sacrifice for it, it has the potential to be done as worship before God: "When I run (or fish, or cook, or read, or paint, or drink coffee), I feel His pleasure." But how do I walk the fine line between worship and idolatry? *"Do not be conformed to this world, but be transformed by the renewal of your mind, that by testing you may discern what is the will of God, what is good and acceptable and perfect." (Romans 12:2)* This is the test that Paul gives to us in order to evaluate the ultimate focus of our worship.

"Do not be conformed..." There have been many sermons preached, classes taught, and books written on what being conformed to this world looks like, and how to avoid it. In the end, they all end up to be a list of do's and don'ts that rarely has anything to do with the heart of God. Paul's admonition has much more to do with the direction of my heart than it does with whether my activities do or don't show up on the list of the "Top Ten Things Good Boys and Girls Do With Their Free Time."

Several years ago, there was a radio show that I really enjoyed. It was broadcast out of Washington D.C., so I couldn't get it over the airwaves in real time, but I was able to download the show from the internet and listen to it at my own pace in the car, during workouts, or just around the house. The show itself was far from sinful—simply an older Jewish radio host commenting on sports and pop culture, along with a few sidekicks and regular guests with outsized, but generally pleasant, personalities. However, according to Paul's definition, it was certainly either a conduit for, *or* a focus of, my worship. I was dedicated to the show, often hurrying back to a computer soon after the show finished in order to download the audio. I would make time to listen, sometimes sacrificing connections, phone calls, or conversations in order to hear the inane conversations each day. However, my regular listening habit kept me abreast of the day's news and happenings, I reasoned, and that would "help" me pray for the world in a more informed way. After all, weren't those that I was ministering to immersed in this same world? I needed to have *some* way of engaging it.

I was not being conformed to the world in a way that could be seen by any outward, observable standard. A radio show hosted by a grumpy Jewish man didn't make any list of taboo activities for Christian men—at least none that I had ever seen or heard about. However, the test wasn't an outward one; it was in my affections. Were my affections for the person of Jesus growing deeper and stronger, or were they plateauing or even fading? Was I being drawn more to the things of God, or more to the things of the world? As I approached the people and things that God had lovingly created and placed in my life, did I tend to see them more from His perspective, or more from my own?

This is the negative side of the test that Paul lays out for us. Does that thing (or person, or activity) that I'm dedicated to and sacrifice for grow my affections for Jesus, or make them stall? If my affections grow, then I am finding myself engaged in worship. However, if my affections are growing cold, I may be dedicated to, and sacrificing for, the wrong thing.

"but be transformed by the renewal of your mind..." Transformation is mysterious and can be very difficult to understand, let alone measure. However, if conformation is the negative side of Paul's test, then transformation is clearly the positive. Transformation is the objective evidence that the Holy Spirit is at work in the life of the believer, manifested through the fruit of the Spirit (Galatians 5:22-23) showing up at some of the most challenging times in life.

It can maybe be most clearly understood like this: When my life intersects with Jesus, something is always generated in that encounter. Transformation is the thing that is generated, and it always looks different. However, it most often falls in line with who I already was before the transformation occurred.

As a teenager, I was always a voracious reader. I famously found a briefcase at a yard sale during the summer preceding my sixth grade year, and was only saved from certain ostracism by my parents who absolutely forbid that I carry it to school. During our summer beach trips, while other kids were reading sci-fi books or comics, I was reading "The Deming Management Method" and learning about Total Quality Management principles as practiced by Japanese auto makers. I'm not defending these things as normal—I'm simply painting a picture of me as my unredeemed teenage self. Don't judge.

It stands to reason, then, that when my life intersected with Jesus, or more accurately, when He intersected with me, I became passionate about studying the things of God. I read the Bible. I read theology. I read Max Lucado. I read Ravi Zacharias. I read Andrew Murray. I read Martin Luther. I read C.S. Lewis. Transformation in me, as with many, didn't fall outside of my natural personality, but flowed directly in line with who I already was. There are several clear biblical illustrations of the same thing: David, the psalmist, was once the shepherd boy who played music for King Saul; Moses, the great leader of the Israel, was once a natural leader in Pharaoh's palace whose "leadership" forced him into a forty-year exile in the desert prior to God's call through the burning bush; and Paul, the master theologian of the early church, was first Saul of Tarsus, the Pharisee and star pupil of Gamaliel.

Whole Life Worship

What does all this mean for worship? Clearly, worship is larger than a corporate or individual activity done once a day or once a week. But it also means that worship can and must take as many forms as there are people! Every activity, every relationship, every passion and personality trait— all are opportunities for the glory of God to be seen. We must recognize that God has uniquely created us just as we are, and it's through being the people we are, transformed by His grace, that God is most glorified in us. This means that vocational ministry isn't the pinnacle of a life given to worship, but just another expression of worship within the broad spectrum.

The plumber or teacher or line worker has just as many opportunities for bringing glory to God as the theologian does.

Eric Liddell glorified God with his speed every bit as much as he did with his service in China. Personally, I seek to glorify God with affections stirred toward Him and a desire to read and learn. Others glorify Him with hands that serve, homes that welcome, minds that create, relationships that nurture, and countless other variations. The form is not the point, but the all-encompassing totality of our worship is. There must be no place in our lives where worship stops and something else begins, for all of our lives belong to Him—we were bought with a price. (1 Corinthians 6:20)

Brennan Manning quotes a letter found on a pastor's desk in Zimbabwe after the pastor had been martyred for his faith.

I'm part of the fellowship of the unashamed. I have the Holy Spirit power. The die has been cast. I have stepped over the line. The decision has been made—I'm a disciple of His. I won't look back, let up, slow down, back away, or be still. My past is redeemed, my present makes sense, my future is secure. I'm finished and done with low living, sight walking, smooth knees, colorless dreams, tamed visions, worldly talking, cheap giving, and dwarfed goals. I no longer need preeminence, prosperity, position, promotions, plaudits, or popularity. I don't have to be right, first, tops, recognized, praised, regarded, or rewarded. I now live by faith, lean in his presence, walk by patience, am uplifted by prayer, and I labor with power. My face is set, my gait is fast, my goal is heaven, my road is narrow, my way rough, my companions are few, my Guide reliable, my mission clear. I cannot be bought, compromised, detoured, lured away, turned back, deluded, or delayed. I will not flinch in the face of sacrifice, hesitate in the presence of the enemy, pander at the pool of popularity, or meander in the maze of mediocrity. I won't give up, shut up, let up, until I have stayed up, stored up, prayed up, paid up, preached up for the cause of Christ. I am a disciple of Jesus. I must go till he comes, give till I drop, preach till all know, and work till he stops me. And, when he comes for his own, he will have no problem recognizing me—my banner will be clear![7]

That, my friends, is worship.

---

7 Quoted in Brennan Manning, *The Signature of Jesus* (Multnomah, Sisters, OR, first published 1988, revised 1996.) pgs. 31-32.

Worship as a Lifestyle
Questions for Reflection

1. When you think of worship, what immediately comes to mind?

2. What's the difference between worshiping to earn the mercy of God versus worshiping in response to His mercy?

3. What are some of the things that you know that you are dedicated to and sacrifice for? Choose two or three, and do the "transformation test" on them. Do they represent areas of worship, or could they be areas of idolatry?

4. Where have you seen the transformation of the Holy Spirit in your life?

5. In his Bible paraphrase called The Message, author Eugene Peterson translates Romans 12:1 like this: *"So here's what I want you to do, God helping you: Take your everyday, ordinary life—your sleeping, eating, going-to-work, and walking-around life—and place it before God as an offering."* Think about your everyday, ordinary life. What's an area that could be offered to God as worship?

CHAPTER THREE
Authentic Community

"The serious Christian, set down for the first time in a Christian community, is likely to bring with him a very definite idea of what Christian life together should be and try to realize it. By sheer grace, God will not permit us to live even for a brief period in [that] dream world. Only that fellowship which faces such disillusionment, with all its unhappy and ugly aspects, begins to be what it should be in God's sight. A community which cannot bear such a crisis, which insists upon keeping its illusion when it should be shattered, permanently loses in that moment the promise of the Christian community. He who loves his dream of a community more than the Christian community itself becomes a destroyer of the latter, even though his personal intentions may be ever so honest and earnest and sacrificial."

- Dietrich Bonhoeffer

"My dad left our family when I was 14." Her voice, amplified through the microphone, filled the sanctuary. It was the Sunday after Easter, and the pastor had asked a few people to share what the cross and their recent journey toward it meant to them. This young woman speaking was in her mid-twenties. Now and again her voice would waver with the emotion of all she was saying, but she spoke confidently and without hesitation.

She continued, "Of course, that meant there were lots of issues that I've dealt with through life, and that I'm still dealing with. I am often wondering when the people who are most important in my life will leave; when good friends will just disappear or turn away from me. But more than anything, I've asked that about Jesus. Of course He *says* He'll never leave me or forsake me, but there's always a question in the back of my mind. If a father would leave his four young kids, wouldn't it be possible that one day Jesus just wouldn't be there anymore? But the great gift that Jesus gave me this Lenten season was a moment of insight. He showed me that it's the cross that tells me He'll never leave. He was on that cross, and if there was anyone ever that could have changed things, He could have. He didn't deserve the punishment He was getting. He said Himself that there were legions of angels just waiting for His command to come and rescue Him. As He hung on that cross, God showed me that He could have left at any time; and, honestly, if He was going to leave, that would have been the time. But He didn't. He stayed. Bearing my sin. Loving me. Sacrificing His life for mine. There are times that I'm afraid that Jesus will leave me alone. But the cross tells me that He never will."

She finished speaking, and the congregation murmured their agreement with what she had learned from God through the Lenten season. Following the service, a family that was attending our church for the first time that morning was blown away by the young woman's story: "In the churches we've attended, we've *never* seen anyone willing to talk publicly about anything like that! It's amazing she would be willing to talk like that."

There's no question that a willingness to be *that* honest before several hundred people is not the typical church experience. Which brings up two questions: first, why *isn't* it typical for members of the body of Christ to be completely honest with one another? And, maybe even more importantly, what made it different for this young lady, along with many other willing individuals to be honest before one another about difficulties and challenges in life?

Masquerade
The scenario is so sadly familiar that it needs little explanation: the morning was chaos as mom and dad try to get the kids dressed and somewhat

cleaned up and ready for church. The last several minutes before they rush out the door are little more than a back and forth volley of frustrated and angry shouts and responses amidst the flurry of activity. The first few minutes of the car ride is icy silence, before one family member finally dares to break the silence. The statement they make, however, doesn't "land" as much as it *detonates* in the middle of the car. The shouting is at full volume once again, which lasts the rest of the way to the church building. It stops mid-sentence, however, as they pull into the church parking lot. Mom and Dad paste on some fake smiles, grip one another's hand (probably a bit too tightly) as they walk across the parking lot toward the smiling greeter at the door.

> **Greeter:** *How are you folks doing this morning?*
> **Father:** *We're doing wonderful, praise the Lord! It's great to be here!*
> *(Mother's smile widens as she nods. The kids trudge past, looking none too happy. That is, unless they're of a certain age... in which case, they may have already learned how to play the "church" game.)*

Sunday morning church, at least when practiced this way, is little more than a masquerade ball. Everyone carefully prepares their masks so that when the party starts, no one will know who they *really* are. They can appear perfect and presentable, as though they have everything all together, at least until the car ride home. The masks stay up, and no one ever knows what lies underneath.

That is, at least, until everything crashes down and the perfect exterior can no longer be maintained. The perfect couple with the perfect marriage gets a not so perfect divorce. The star student gets arrested. The Elder's wife finally breaks and talks about an abusive pattern in her marriage. A computer virus uncovers the pastor's pornography addiction. The women's ministry leader checks into rehab after a surprise DUI checkpoint reveals a twenty year alcohol problem. The shiny veneer, no longer able to be maintained, comes crashing down—far too late for the body of Christ to do anything except help to pick up the pieces. The real question is: Why? Why fake it? Why continue the masquerade?

The Dead End Cycle

Each of us would probably use a slightly different term to name our reasons for doing it. There are those that would label it "acceptance" or "significance" or plain and simple "affection." Some might even use the term "community," which is, admittedly, somewhat of a buzz word these days. The bottom line is that we fake it so that *we can get what we long for*—love. In the end, we all want to be loved, and we're constantly willing to do what it takes to "qualify" for that love.

Consider this: The woman that hides her drinking problem inside the walls of the church will likely exaggerate it at her AA meeting. Why? Just because it's more acceptable? Not at all! For the same reason she hides it in the church! She wants to be loved and accepted, and in the setting of the AA meeting, being a drunk will get her there, so she exaggerates her drunkenness. In the setting of the church, being perfect will get her there, so she'll pretend to be perfect. Either way, she pretends as though she's something that she's not in order to get something that she wants.

It's at just this point the cycle breaks down. When this mythical woman puts on her mask, whether it's in the church setting or somewhere else, and pretends that she's the person that she thinks those around her want her to be, she is really seeking the love of those in that community. However, once she actually gets that love, the deep recesses of her heart and mind start to plague her. Consciously or unconsciously, she begins to recognize that these people don't truly love *her*. The love feels nice on the outside, but it is hollow and dissatisfying in the depth of her heart because she recognizes that the person they love doesn't even really exist. She's a made up person. A figment of her imagination. The cycle might look like this (Figure 3.1):

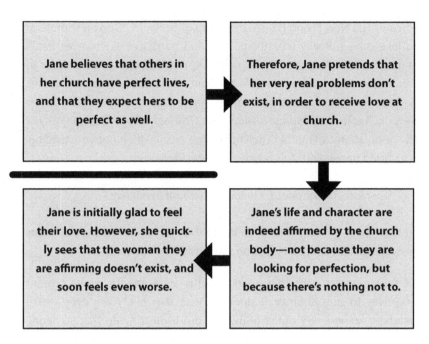

Figure 3.1

Worse yet, she can no longer give real love either, because she's now entered a desperate search for love and acceptance. Every word and action is working toward that end goal. People are no longer creations of God, bearing His image, to be loved and affirmed; rather, they are puzzle pieces that she is trying to arrange in order to meet her own needs. Jane might express love to a certain person at a certain point in time, but when that person no longer fits into the puzzle, they are discarded, and she moves on.

The masquerade is a dead end.

Love Without Hypocrisy

It's once again in the twelfth chapter of his letter to Roman Christians that the apostle Paul gives us insight into this struggle. His admonition is this: "Let love be genuine." (Romans 12:9a, ESV) The NIV states: "Love must be sincere." The New Living is even more straightforward: "Don't just pretend to love others. Really love them." All good translations. However, Paul's statement is really made in the negative, not in the positive, and it's in this nuance that we begin to see the light at the end of this dark tunnel. Perhaps the most accurate translation can be found in the Old King James Version: "Let love be *without dissimilation*." The fact that the vast majority of the population can neither spell nor define *dissimilation* notwithstanding, it's a good translation! This is what Paul literally says:

*"Your love for one another should be **without hypocrisy**."*

At least that's the way it reads in the BKV (Brian Kannel Version, all rights reserved). No hypocrisy. No faking. No masks. The real deal.

Of course, that means that we're called to be authentic as we present ourselves to one another. It doesn't mean that everyone, everywhere needs to know every detail of my life, but it *must* mean that someone does, and that someone (or those several some*ones*) should be within my local community of faith. That insures that the local body of Christ (Paul's subject in Romans 12) is a place where love is without hypocrisy. It also means that even for those who aren't privy to every detail of my life, I'm still not seeking to present an image of myself that's not true. I'm not trying to impress you, and you shouldn't be trying to impress me. We're together relishing the grace given to us by Jesus exactly where we are.

But "love without hypocrisy" also has another, even more uncomfortable, dynamic. If you and I are to be authentic in our community, I can't be willing to pretend that you're something you're not just as I can't pretend to be something that *I'm* not. Each of us needs to be willing to lovingly confront those in our inner circle with holes that we see in each other's lives, challenging blatant sin and even direction toward sin. This might mean some extremely uncomfortable conversations, some tense discussions, and intentional relationships that strain under the weight of real community.

There will be some who hear this call to authenticity and quietly decide to remain on the outside. "If I don't engage deeply and don't let anyone truly see inside my life," they might reason, "I won't have to really fake it, but I can still hide." Here's the problem: Spiritual growth and the fullness of life that Jesus promises to us is *inextricably linked* to a deep connection to the community. Passages like 1 Corinthians 12-14, Galatians 6:1-5, Ephesians 4:1-16, Hebrews 10:24-25, as well as many others, point to this reality. Therefore, a decision to stay on the sideline might protect our secrets from a few, but the trade-off is a loss of joy, distance from God, a lack of transformation, and ultimately, missing out of the love that you are designed to receive. Without authentic community, we get stuck.

Two Kinds of Stuck

It stands to reason that the pursuit of the Almighty God would need to occur on His terms. He has wired us a certain way, and He has laid out our spiritual journey with certain non-negotiables present within it. One of those non-negotiables is the presence and involvement of an authentic community. This is the way the writer to Hebrews spells it out for us: "Take care, brothers, lest there be in any of you an evil, unbelieving heart, leading you to fall away from the living God. But exhort one another every day, as long as it is called 'today,' that none of you may be hardened by the deceitfulness of sin." (Hebrews 3:12-13) It's imperative, then, that we exhort one another within the community around us—otherwise, we may develop evil, hard, and unbelieving hearts! The stakes are high.

However, we can't simply be connected to a community. Simply being present within a local body not only doesn't move our hearts forward in Christ-likeness, it can lull us into believing that we are really OK when we're really not. After all, we're a part of the "church" aren't we? However, there are countless people who are integrally involved in the "church," but never truly engage the community of the church. They're stuck.

Stuck by Internalizing
One error that we can often make in community is by internalizing our spiritual journey. This happens every time that we decide we'll be honest in our spiritual struggle—as soon as that struggle becomes a victory.

Maybe the most dramatic difference between someone who has recently come to faith in Jesus and someone who has been a disciple of Jesus for a long time is the way that each handles their sinfulness. When a man first comes to faith, he's completely open and honest about his sin and the baggage that he brings along on his faith journey. In fact, it doesn't even feel like baggage to him—it's just real life! There's recognition that, in many areas, his life is out of sync with the life of Christ. This isn't a cause for shame or for hiding areas of life—it's simply reality of life in the world. One of my greatest joys as a pastor is to walk alongside such new believers in their journeys. While I'm certainly not a proponent of crude language or immoral behavior, it's incredibly refreshing to have a young man unpack his very real life to me using the only language that he knows, not avoiding certain words or subjects because he's "talking to the pastor." It's in the brutal honesty of these early discussions that truly exponential growth in the Spirit begins to happen. Nothing is hidden, and the Lordship of Jesus rightfully extends into every area of life.

However, somewhere down the line, that changes. For some, it only takes a few weeks. For others, months or years. But at some point, the lie begins to creep in: Everyone, including Jesus, expects you to be better than you really are. The behavior that was once recognized as a natural consequence of a fallen world and brought into the light so that it could be forgiven and healed is now hidden. Spiritual growth has become internalized.

The process goes something like this: A young man finds himself in the midst of sinful thoughts or behavior. He "knows better", but can't seem to win the battle against his sinful nature (which is, by the way, the exact situation that the apostle Paul described of himself near the end of his life in Romans 7:15-24!). However, rather than bring this struggle into the light, he takes the truth that he knows along with his own struggle with sin, and hides it in the "back room" of his life. He's working on it, he reasons, and when he's found victory—or at least some victory—he'll share the story so that he can be an encouragement to his other brothers who might be struggling in the same way. However, if he would share the struggle in the midst of it, what would they say? What would they think?

However, by this very process, he removes the reality of his spiritual journey from the community. He takes a spiritual practice that was always meant to be communal and, instead, makes it individual. At best, his spiritual growth stalls as he wrestles with sin for weeks, months, or even years. At worse, he gets trapped in bondage and never again experiences the joy and freedom that God has intended for him to live within. He's stuck.

Stuck by Institutionalizing

Pop quiz: What happened in 313 A.D.? And what does it have to do with your spiritual life today?

The answer actually has incredible implications for the way that we follow Jesus today. In 313 A.D., Emperors Constantine and Licinious signed the Edict of Milan, which gave religious tolerance and freedom to Christians within the Roman Empire. Why does that matter to us in 21st century North America? Up until 313, Christianity was a persecuted movement of people who risked everything to follow Jesus. Joining the church cost something. In some cases, it cost everything. But in 313 A.D., for the first time ever, you could walk down the aisle of your local cathedral and shake the hand of the priest who would welcome you into the fellowship and invite you to the next covered-dish supper. No real cost. Very minimal commitment. For the first time in history, you could be a *member* without ever intending to be a disciple.

Ever since, at least in the vast majority of the Western world, this has been a constant temptation. "Church" has become a title for a building, not for a group of people. Affirmation of doctrine has replaced life transformation.

A defined set of rules and expectations has co-opted the messiness of a life led by the Holy Spirit. Or, at least, the possibility for these things are often there. Author Mark Buchannan says it well:

> "At some point we stopped calling Christians disciples and started calling them believers. A disciple is one who follows and imitates Jesus. She loses her life in order to find it. A believer, not so. She holds certain beliefs, but how deep down these go depends on the weather or her mood. She can get defensive, sometimes bristlingly so, about her beliefs, but in her honest moments she wonders why they've made such scant difference... You can't be a disciple without being a believer. But—here's the rub—you can be a believer and not a disciple. You can say all the right things, think all the right things, believe all the right things, do all the right things, and still not follow and imitate Jesus."[8]

The option of membership without cost, belief without conviction, connection without transformation—it leaves us in a very precarious position. "Community" must never simply mean a group of people with whom we are simply affiliated. When lives are simply connected but not truly shared, spiritual growth is institutionalized. We're stuck.

OK not to be OK

So, how do we enter into authentic community? How does a church become a place where a twenty-something young woman is willing to talk in front of a full congregation about the challenges and fears that come with having a father that abandoned her?

It's vital that the church be a place where it's OK not to be OK. For everyone. From the brand new believer to the pastor or the long-time Elder. But most importantly, for *you*. And for me.

---

8 Mark Buchannan, *Your Church is Too Safe*, (Zondervan, Grand Rapids, MI., 2012) Kindle location 794-803.

Churches are often places that are very accepting of the brokenness of others. In the cycle above (Figure 2.1), Jane *believed* that everyone's lives were perfect, and she *believed* that everyone expected that hers would be as well. However, apart from some extreme cases, most church bodies have an incredible capacity for grace, particularly as it relates to someone who is broken and repentant about her sin. It's likely that Jane's beliefs were not well-founded, and that, if she had been willing to be authentically herself, without hypocrisy, she would have been accepted and loved exactly as she is. And I believer, dear reader, that *you* would have accepted and loved her. As would have I.

But that doesn't mean that either of us would have been willing to test out that grace ourselves. We're like the man who owns just about every tool that's ever been produced and will gladly loan them out to any of his neighbors that are in need of them. However, when he finds himself missing the necessary tool for the project that he's working on, he goes out and buys one himself, although he's well aware that Fred next door has that exact tool hanging in his shed. Why not walk over and ask Fred? He's very willing to loan his tools to anyone, but he would never think of borrowing himself.

Many of us find ourselves in the same position with grace. We're quite willing to extend it, but completely unwilling to ask for it. We would rather pretend, or more accurately stated, lie than ask for grace in our brokenness. Instead, we maintain the façade, and hope that it doesn't fall down. And as long as grace is truly amazing for everyone except for you and I, the church will never be a place where it's OK not to be OK.

The problem with that is that what is lost is the very heart of the gospel itself. The gospel boldly states that our righteousness can never be found within ourselves but only ever in Christ, by faith in Him. Following the law, while certainly a pathway to our joy, has no power to give us right-standing. *At the point which the law, whether the biblical law or a set of sub-cultural standards that develop as acceptable practice within the church, becomes a way by which we evaluate one another or even our own lives, the gospel is lost.* I would encourage you to read that last sentence again. Once there is a standard apart from Jesus Himself, the gospel disappears. Therefore, my sin is absolutely a barrier to the fullness of joy that Jesus offers to me, but it's *never* a reason for shame, *never* something to be hidden, and *never* a standard by which I'm measured or by which I may measure anyone else. The church, of all places on earth, must be a place where it's OK not to be OK.

Of course, that doesn't mean that we are to stay there. Through the transformation of the Holy Spirit within us, and through the love and encouragement of one another, we are constantly being made more like Jesus. However, pretending to be more like Him than we actually are not only doesn't accomplish that transformation, it actually gets in the way. That's really the point of the hourglass: Through every area of my life being offered in worship and by taking off the mask and being real with a community of believers who are also committed to moving toward Jesus, we put ourselves in a position to be transformed by the ongoing work of the Holy Spirit. There's one final ingredient that makes up the environment for transformation—the foundation on which all of this is built. That's for the next chapter.

Authentic Community
Questions for Reflection

1. What are some areas of your life in which you tend to be less than authentic with those in the body of Christ?

2. Have you ever experienced spiritual growth as a communal process? For instance, has a particular community ever had a profound effect on your spiritual growth (positively or negatively)?

3. In what areas do you tend to internalize your spiritual growth? Who are some people that you could intentionally invite into that process?

4. Have areas of belief become institutionalized for you—have you made mental assent to a specific truth, but are unwilling to live as though that is true? What are some steps that you can take to bring belief and action in line with one another?

5. How could the short-term pain of being brutally honest about your short-comings with the community around you bring the long-term joy of transformation in your life?

CHAPTER FOUR
The Foundation of the Word

"Our aim in studying the Godhead must be to know God himself better. Our concern must be to enlarge our acquaintance, not simply with the doctrine of God's attributes, but with the living God whose attributes they are. It was for this purpose that revelation was given, and it is to this use that we must put it."
- J.I. Packer

In November 1989, an architecturally fascinating new building opened up on the campus of The Ohio State University. The Wexner Center for the Arts uses various forms of architecture, including the use of hundreds of white grid pieces, which all seem to evoke a sense of dizziness and confusion. Visitors have even reported a sense of nausea at times as they wandered the angled hallways and made their way through sidewalk passageways. Architect Peter Eisenman designed the building according to his deconstructionist preferences, and the result can be disorienting if not at times downright maddening.

In a critique of post-modern culture and thinking, Dr. Ravi Zacharias makes the following observation:

> An utterly fascinating illustration of this duping of ourselves is the latest arts building opened at Ohio State University, the Wexner Center for the Arts, another one of our chimerical *(definition: product of an unchecked imagination)* exploits in the

name of intellectual advance. Newsweek branded this building "America's first deconstructionist building." Its white scaffolding, red brick turrets, and Colorado grass pods evoke a double take. But puzzlement only intensifies when you enter the building, for inside you encounter stairways that go nowhere, pillars that hang from the ceiling without purpose, and angled surfaces configured to create a sense of vertigo. The architect, we are duly informed, designed this building to reflect life itself—senseless and incoherent—and the "capriciousness of the rules that organize the built world." When the rationale was explained to me, I had just one question: Did he do the same with the foundation? *(definition added)*

In his disarming observation, Dr. Zacharias reminds us of what we know is true: a structure, whatever it is made out of or made to look like, is dependent upon its foundation for support, strength, and stability. If the foundation is faulty, the building is doomed, but if the foundation is solid and secure, even the most unlikely building can stand.

The Word as Foundation

Increasingly, the authority of the Scriptures is under attack. Sadly, it is no longer even unusual or surprising to hear an ordained minister within certain streams of the church declare that there are huge sections of the Bible that they don't consider to be true. In fact, the idea of truth that is universally true (meaning that certain truths simply *are* true regardless of time, place, circumstance, experience, or situation) can no longer be assumed in many circles. While it's certainly a topic that merits significant discussion, that discussion is outside the scope of this book. York Alliance Church falls squarely in the stream of the Christian church known as "evangelicalism" which, for all of its strengths and weaknesses, has traditionally been strong in its focus on the Word of God. Most of those who are reading this book would quickly affirm that Bible plays a vital role in the life of a believer, and it is the only adequate foundation on which to build the church.[9]

The question is, however, what does that really mean? How does one make the Word of God the foundation of their life? How is a church built on the foundation of the Word?

How We View the Word

Do you remember the "Rubik's cube?" When I was growing up in the 80's, it was one of the hottest toys on the market. Basically, it was a cube with nine movable squares on each of its six sides. Each square was a color—six colors total, and every color had nine squares. (Figure 4.1)

The goal was to get all six sides to be solid colors. Simple, right? But it could be turned tons of different directions, and, once the colors were messed up, it seemed to be impossible to get them back where they should go. At least it was for me.

Figure 4.1

Our life in Christ bears many similarities to the Rubik's cube. We come to faith, and it feels like Jesus has done all of the twisting and turning necessary to get all of the colors on all of the right sides. We feel great—put together just right. However, it's not long (minutes? hours?) until something happens, the first twist is made, and the perfection is messed up. I'm tempted into sin and, rather than resist, I give in. I lose my job. Friends get upset with me. I have family problems. A close relative gets sick. My kid gets in trouble. It could be any number of things that cause it, but the end result is that the colors are no longer where they're supposed to be. I'm messed up.

---

9 Some may feel that this is in opposition to Paul's teaching in 1 Corinthians 3:10-11, where he clearly states that Jesus Himself is the foundation of the church. Hopefully the rest of the chapter will explain how these two statements are not only not contradictory, but that the statement made above is actually affirming the truth of 1 Corinthians 3.

And so, I bring my messed up self to the Word, hoping to get fixed. I'm struggling with sin, so I read 1 John, then Psalm 51, then memorize 1 Corinthians 10:13 and begin repeating it like a mantra. Turn left, then right, then left again. And, sometimes, by the grace of God, it actually works! I've used my concordance, found the right Scriptures, read them, and I feel better. I've won at Bible roulette—you know, the game of chance where you randomly open your Bible to a page and read the first thing your eye settles on, hoping it's not Matthew 27:5. ("And throwing down the pieces of silver into the temple, [Judas] departed, and he went and hanged himself.") I've come to the Word to fix me, and now I'm feeling better. I'm acting better. I'm fixed.

Of course, when this method actually works, I ultimately have an even bigger problem. The next time a problem hits (say, a parent's sickness or job loss), I come back to the Word and do the same thing. This time, it's Isaiah 53, Jeremiah 29:11, John 16:23-24. I'm reading, memorizing, praying, naming, and claiming. But this time, it doesn't work. I still feel lousy. The problem's still there. My attitude not only didn't get better, it actually got worse. What happened? Why didn't it work?

It didn't work because God never intended the Bible to be used that way. That's not why He gave it to us. And that's *not* what it means to build a life on the foundation of the Word. The Word of God has never claimed to be a magic formula, God's "rule book", a roadmap for living, or any of the other things that we call on it to be, and, when we approach it that way, we get frustrated because it doesn't come through like we feel like it should.

So what happens then? Unless you were a child prodigy, you probably reached that point of frustration with the Rubik's cube. (I know I did!) One of two responses typically happened—or maybe, like me, you did a little of both.

Putting it on the shelf
Once I tried and tried and couldn't solve it, I just gave up. I can still picture my Rubik's cube sitting in the corner of the little brown desk in my room,

gathering dust. No point in picking it up, since I couldn't solve it anyway! It just sat there.

The parallel is obvious. When I come to the Word like a solution to the problems of my life and it doesn't work, I get frustrated. Again and again, I come to the Word, doing what I think I'm supposed to do, but come away dissatisfied because my problem is still just as present as it was before I picked up the Bible. So, after a while, I just stop.

We live in an age where there are more versions of the Bible translated, more study helps published, more materials available, more teaching broadcast, and more conferences held than at any time in history. Do you know what other statistical category the Western church is leading history in? Biblical ignorance among the average church member. With everything that's available to us, we're more ignorant than ever. Most church-going Americans own between 3 and 5 Bibles. There are many reading this book that are well into double-digit Bible ownership. So why don't we know the Word? Because, like my old Rubik's cube, it's been put on the shelf. For some, that's a literal reality: My six Bibles are carefully placed in strategic locations, but they only move when I need to carry them to church or to a LIFE group meeting. For others, this is much more of a figurative reality: The Bible is read, often "religiously" to use a pun, but I'm not really engaging it. I read the Word each morning because it gives me a good start to the day, but I don't actually remember what I'm reading, nor do I ever make the jump of applying it to real life. The Word is compartmentalized into the "church" box and, if I'm totally honest, the "church" box has very little to do with the rest of my life.

The Bible is on the shelf.

Peeling stickers

I have a little tinge of OCD. OK, it's not truly diagnosed, but it's pretty easy to see that it's there. In fact, those who know me well would likely say that describing it as a "tinge" is a "tinge" too gracious. The bottom line is this:

There was no way that a messed up Rubik's cube could sit on the corner of my desk for too long without being fixed. It was driving me crazy. I talked to my friends—could they fix it? They were as frustrated as me. Since this was before the internet, I couldn't Google the solution (although, I can *now*, and after reading *and* watching the video, I still can't do it). So, I did what just about every self-respecting teenager of the 80's did—I peeled off the stickers.

One day, armed with my pocket knife and the most precision my 13 year-old body could muster, I "fixed" it. I took off each sticker, one by one, and moved it to the right place. Of course, the problem was that they weren't actually in the right place—underneath, the cube wasn't fixed at all. But it looked better. And, by golly, that's all that mattered.

Again, the parallel comes quite easily. In chapter 2 we looked at Paul's admonition to the Romans that they should not be conformed but, rather, transformed. (Romans 12:1-2) It's not an outward process but, rather, an inside-out process. In another letter, Paul states clearly that righteousness does not come from us, but that it comes from Him. (Philippians 3:7-10) In yet another letter, he declares that it's only by grace that we are saved, not by anything we can do. (Ephesians 2:8-9) Looking good on the outside while still being messed up on the inside has no value whatsoever.

Us sticker-peelers do tend to know the Word pretty well. Or at least we know a lot of verses. Rarely do we understand the context for those verses or the heart of God behind those verses, but we definitely know the verses. In fact, we'll quote them, loudly and boldly, to anyone who will listen, but particularly to those who, in our sacred opinion, are violating them. All the while, we find ourselves hanging on to outward holiness with all of the white-knuckled intensity of a 10 year-old boy on his first roller coaster ride, afraid that, if we let go, we'll slip hopelessly in the oblivion of the pagan world around us. Sticker-peelers know that Jesus said to be in the world but not of the world (John 17:14-16), but rather than doing the difficult wrestling with the Holy Spirit that's required to work that out in real life, we would rather yell at the world for being worldly. Loudly protest worldliness. Try to get anti-worldliness legislation passed. All of which is akin to being angry at the darkness because it's so… well… dark.

Sticker-peelers, of course, have foolproof reasoning for why they do what they do. The short version of the story is really no different than my Rubick's cube story: I tried, but it didn't work. If it was ever going to be solved, I needed to resort to desperate measures. Maybe other people can do it, which is great for them, but as for me, peeling stickers was the only option. Unless, of course, I just left it on the shelf.

How the Bible Views the Word

When we approach the Bible as though it contains a magic spell, the recipe for a good life, the solution to our problems, or the road map for living, we'll ultimately be disappointed because we won't find what we're looking for there (unless, of course, you're looking for a map of the divided Kingdom of Israel in 723 B.C., which should show up in the back of some reference Bibles). We won't find these things because that's not why God has given the Word to us, and it's not what the Bible itself claims to be!

The question, then, is why *did* God give us the Word, and how are we supposed to build our lives on it? The gospel of John opens with these words: "In the beginning was the Word, and the Word was with God, and the Word was God. *He* was in the beginning with God." (John 1:1-2, italics mine) So it seems that the Bible is trying to tell us that "the Word" is not a concept, a philosophical idea, or a religious system of behavior, but the Word is actually *a person*. The Bible, then, isn't simply a set of prescribed rules and strange stories, but rather, a revelation of the nature and character of that Person. Within its pages, I may or may not find an easy answer to my suffering, but I'll definitely find the heart of the Word towards my suffering. I may or may not find the specific next step that I should be taking in life, but I'll definitely find that there is One who knows my steps, and who lovingly guides me.

Well, that changes things! Since I'm a person (and I'm assuming by the fact that you're still reading this book to this point, you likely are as well), I can begin to see a bit of the issue with the Rubick's cube model. What is my reaction to another person who only ever comes to me with problems to be solved and burdens to be removed? While I may or may not be willing and able to meet those needs, that type of a relationship is going to have a very limited chance at depth and intimacy. If the Word is a person, I need to change my approach!

Approaching the Word

John declares at the outset of his gospel that Jesus is the Word. Through the rest of the gospel account, Jesus makes seven "I Am" statements that give a clear window into who He is and how we are to approach Him.

I Am the Bread of Life. *(John 6:35)*

Jesus declares that He is sustenance for us. When responding to Satan's temptation to turn stones into bread in the midst of His extreme hunger, Jesus quotes Deuteronomy by saying "Man shall not live by bread alone, but by every word that comes from the mouth of God." (Matthew 4:4) We should approach the Word as we approach food—regularly, hungrily, gratefully.

I Am the Light of the World. *(John 8:12)*

The Word shines light into darkness, and by doing so, helps us to see. Interestingly, the psalmist says nearly the same thing about the Word as he understood it: "Your Word is a lamp to my feet and a light to my path." (Psalm 119:105) As we sit under the teaching of the Word, we're able to make sense out of some of the darkness around us. And Jesus tells us that, once that happens, you and I become the light of the world as well! (Matthew 5:14)

I Am the Door of the sheep. *(John 10:7)*

Jesus is the entry point for real life. He invites us into the sheepfold where we can experience joy and freedom under His Lordship, but He is the only way into that life. He states quite clearly in the same passage that any who gain entry another way are wolves and thieves, not shepherds or sheep.

I Am the Good Shepherd. *(John 10:11)*
He's not just the entryway into that life, but He's the guide for it. Just like that which a shepherd provides, we will sometimes find that the Word has marked out a very clear path for us. However, at other times, we will have a vast field to enjoy. In either case, the Shepherd is going before us, turning over stones, warning of danger, and clearing the paths before us.

I Am the Resurrection and the Life. *(John 11:25)*
Death is the ultimate enemy. Jesus, in love for us and out of an abundance of grace towards us, has conquered that enemy. The Word describes this One who has loved us so much that He would conquer death and give us life in its place, even at incredible personal cost.

I Am the Way, the Truth, and the Life. *(John 14:6)*
Jesus clearly declares that He is the only way to the Father. The Word declares the heart of God in making us, calling us, remaining faithful to us, and redeeming us, and then calling us out into the world to join Him in that redemptive process. When we approach the Word, we hear that heart and receive greater understanding of what it means for Him to love us.

I Am the true Vine. *(John 15:1)*
It's only from the vine that fruit will come. Jesus declares that He is the vine and that fruit is produced in and through Him. We approach the Word out of a desire to remain in the vine and, as we do, our lives will bear fruit. Fruit doesn't come from a behavioral standard or a philosophical belief but, rather, from the Person of the Word at work within us.

These "I Am" statements act like ropes, graciously thrown down from God, on which we can start to ascend to a greater understanding of who He is. The names and concepts in no way *contain* Him, but they absolutely describe a portion of Him, and they give us a way to grab hold.

Wells and Fences

The Australian outback is full of massive cattle ranches. They are so large that fencing them in is literally an impossibility, both from a cost and labor perspective. Millions of head of cattle roam the fields, yet, even without fences, they never wander away from their owner's property. Why is that? Years ago, ranchers figured out the secret: If they sunk wells in the center of the property, the cattle would always remain relatively close. If they got too far from the center of the property, there was no longer any water. Therefore, as they wandered, they would get thirsty and would come back to the center.[10] This is a beautiful picture of Jesus as the Word. In Him we have life. If we spend all of our time and resources building and maintaining a fence at the outskirts of the property, we get desperately thirsty; but, if we stay close to the well, we'll find our lives (and our church) built on the foundation of the Word.

---

10 Michael Frost and Alan Hirsch in *The Shaping of Things to Come*, quoted by Jim Belcher, Deep Church (IVP, Downer's Grove, IL, 2009), pg. 86.

The Foundation of the Word
Questions for Reflection

1. Have you ever struggled to read the Word? Have you ever *not* struggled to read it? What might be the difference?

2. Does it change your approach to the Bible when you see it as the revelation of Jesus to us?

3. Have you put the Word on the shelf? What are some ways that you can more fully engage in the Word and apply it to your life?

4. Which of the seven "I Am" statements hits you most directly at this point in your life? Why?

5. In your reading and application of the Word, do you tend to focus more on the well or the fences?

6. Take a few days and read the entire gospel of John. Pay attention to what Jesus says and does. What surprises you about Him? What puzzles you? What do you like best about Him? Why frustrates you about Him? How do you respond to Him?

CHAPTER FIVE
Prayer as the First Work

"The how-to sermon created a how-to Christianity that is the last dull step of a church that has lost its voice of praise. Rapture needs to reclaim its place in the dull, procedural life of the church. We need to awaken our souls once again. I weary of the repetitive choruses or Christian mantras of our worship that serve to numb our minds rather than to engage them. I weary of sermons that celebrate where we are spiritually rather than enticing us to new vistas of thought and usefulness."

- Calvin Miller

"Don't stop doing any of it." Even as I said the words, I recognized the risk of them. I was sitting across the table from a man who had just recently come to faith in Jesus. His life had been a messy one: a fundamentalist, legalistic upbringing that consisted of being in the church building whenever it was open, but one in which he saw very little evidence of real transformation. In his late teens, he found the temporary peace of his first addiction, and things started to spiral from there. For a period of time he lived a double life: church boy by day, bad boy by night. However, soon, the pretending got old and the church portion was discarded altogether. Life under his own lordship had produced more than a decade of problems, from broken relationships and dead end jobs, to increasing addictions and lifestyle choices that left him often feeling hopeless. It was in the midst of that hopelessness that his real spiritual journey began.

After a few weeks of searching in various places and in various ways, he had scheduled an appointment with a Buddhist monk to discuss the path to enlightenment. However, just three days before the appointment, through the divine work of the Holy Spirit, he became completely aware of the reality of Jesus' life, death, and resurrection. The stories that he had heard for years and knew backward and forward suddenly, in a moment, became real. He was convicted, cut to the core—changed. And so, he showed up in church early on a Sunday morning, we talked, and it was just a day later, in lieu of the meeting with the Buddhist monk, I suppose, that I was having lunch with him.

The entire thing was glorious. He was passionate about following Jesus, ready to do whatever it took to pursue Him. He knew that Jesus was real and that He had saved him. However, there was one problem—the *rest* of his life. The insertion of Jesus didn't change the multiple addictions of which he was still in the throes. It didn't change his relationship with his live-in girlfriend, her son from another relationship and the son they had together, to both of whom he was the only "dad" that they had ever known. It didn't change the network of friendships and relationships that largely revolved around activities that don't typically happen in church fellowship halls. In short, it was all quite messy.

Adding further complication was the fact that he already knew all the rules. Almost two decades of fundamentalist indoctrination had given him a set of rules that would have made the Pharisees proud. He knew what he needed to stop doing, start doing, who he should and shouldn't be with, how much to give, what movies were on the bad list (everything rated R that isn't about Jesus' crucifixion) and which ones were permissible but not beneficial (every other movie that had ever been made except for "Facing the Giants"), the right and wrong radio stations, beverages, and card games. He knew his stuff. And I knew that, if he tried to follow the list of rules, he could never possibly succeed. It wasn't that most of the "list" wasn't the right stuff—it was just that, by trying to conform his life to a list of regulations prior to the transformational work of Jesus leading him there, he was setting himself up for failure and frustration, and, ultimately, for walking away from his newfound faith.

And so, as he described his current life to me, I took a risk: "Don't stop doing any of it. Just pursue Jesus. Spend time in the Word and in prayer, get connected to a small LIFE group community and make sure that you have at least daily contact with other believers. Try to separate this newfound relationship with Jesus from all of the rules that you learned. And when Jesus tells you to stop doing something or start doing something else, follow Him—not because of a rule that you learned, but because He's leading you that way. You'll find that He will have already given you the strength that you need to do it, and has worked out all of the details." Then I ferociously prayed for months that Jesus would indeed do that. Up until that moment, I had never anticipated that good pastoral counsel would be to continue in addictive behaviors and immoral relationships, and frankly, I was petrified myself of what I had just said. I could already envision the conversation with the Elders that would lead to my dismissal: "You told him to do *what*??" However, as I read the pages of the New Testament, that seemed like the business that Jesus had always been in. So, as strange as it sounded to my 21st century church ears, I had at least a sliver of faith that Jesus would come through.

You Foolish Galatians!
Paul's letter to the church in Galatia is a fascinating study of conformation versus transformation. This group of believers had come to Christ and were transformed. They were changed in glorious ways by the person and presence of Jesus. And then, they started following the rules. And making up new ones. And holding each other to this new standard. It would have been silly if it hadn't been such a heresy against the free grace of Jesus. Religious legalism might be defined as seeking to earn what is given for free, and Paul's letter provides insight into one of the early church discipline cases around legalism with which he indicts basically in the entire church. His core argument can be summarized through the end of chapter two and the beginning of chapter three of Galatians:

> "For through the law I died to the law, so that I might live to God. I have been crucified with Christ. It is no longer I who live, but Christ who lives in me. And the life I now live in the flesh I live by faith in the Son of God, who loved me and gave himself for me. I do not nullify the grace of God, for if righteousness were through the law, then Christ died for no purpose. O foolish Galatians! Who has bewitched you? It was before your eyes that Jesus Christ was publicly portrayed as crucified. Let me ask you only this: Did you receive the Spirit by works of the law or by hearing with faith? Are you so foolish? Having begun by the Spirit, are you now being perfected by the flesh?" (Galatians 2:19 – 3:3)

Salvation, Paul clearly states elsewhere, is by grace alone through faith alone. It seems that he's teaching that sanctification (the process of being made holy subsequent to salvation) is equally so—by grace alone through faith alone. In the same way that salvation comes to us as a work of grace, our spiritual growth is His work as well. Of course, like salvation, there is an aspect of the response to that work that falls to us, but the *first* work is His, not ours.

Prayer as the First Work
This brief phrase is the only carryover from the YAC Vision Statement to the Family Values. Our vision ends with the declaration that "in all of this, prayer is the first work", and in the very center of the hourglass, we find the same declaration. The reason for the duplication is simple: While there is work into which we're invited, the core work of the church, along with the core work of discipleship, is His work, not our work. In both cases, the "work" assigned to us is far more passive than active—the work of prayer. We depend upon God to do what we are unable to do on our own.

I'm not much of a handyman, but there are times (far less of them than my wife would like) where I attempt to do projects around the house. I've installed ceiling fans, replaced outlets and switches, and built a few things here and there. Nothing exciting. However, somehow my kids decided that

I had the ability to build things, and so, a few weeks ago, I was accosted as I came through the door with requests to build a clubhouse fort. Their mother had kindly helped them do lots of research on the internet, and they had a plan: In the corner of the yard, using the fence as two of the walls (which wasn't exactly straight to begin with—another project of mine), we would build two additional walls and, *viola*, they would have a fort.

So, "we" measured the area, evaluated the slope of the ground, and got a rough idea of the materials we would need. By "we," of course, I mean *me* using the tape measure to get a general idea of what would be necessary and creating a plan in my head, and my 11-year old daughter and three sons (ages 9, 6, and 3) running chaotically in circles around me, grabbing the end of the tape measure right before I had the measurement I needed, putting folding chairs "inside" the fort that had not yet been built, and generally having a blast. Once I had an idea of what materials were needed, "we" loaded up in the car and drove to the local lumber yard. As "we" arrived at the store, the kids took turns pretending to be boards and pieces of plywood as they rode along on the lumber cart, sitting squarely on the sticker that said "ABSOLUTELY NO RIDING ON THIS CART." "We" then loaded boards and lattice pieces on the cart, meaning that I loaded them on while they counted wrong and then rammed the end of one of the boards into the head of the 3-year old, which created a series of screams that likely resulted in a "C.S.I. York" team being dispatched from downtown and in a waterfall of tears which gave his face that lovely, dirt-streaked, my-pathetic-father-doesn't-know-how-to-give-me-a-bath   look.   "We" moved to the check-out and paid, which of course means that my wallet was lighter and the four of them had very little concept of what happened apart from distracting the dirty, streak-faced boy so that we could load the car before the private investigator showed up.

"We" then made it home and began the work of creating the structure itself. The kids armed themselves with small hammers while I made the necessary cuts with the power saw. "We" put the framing together, which consisted of me desperately trying to find small tasks for the kids to do so that I could get the wood screwed together without seriously injuring anyone. Once the frames were together, the kids used their little hammers to nail the lattice work on the frames, a project I could have easily done in five minutes, but gladly took the 30-minute break as they beat on the wood, got distracted and wandered away and back again, hit a few thumbs (mostly their own, but in one odd circumstance, the 3-year old's thumb ended up under the hammer of the 9-year old, which resulted in more C.S.I.-level screaming), and finally got the lattice mostly attached to the frames. "We" then installed the walls in their proper places, much to the excitement of the entire team—although, to be fair, the motivation for my excitement was far different than theirs. "We" had *together* built a fort, and they were thrilled.

Believe it or not, this is a picture of prayer in action. God, our loving and patient Father, invites us into His work. In fact, He refuses to do it without us. It's not that He's unable to do it without us—it goes without saying that He's far more capable of doing the work that He is doing in the world around us on His own than I'll ever be at building a fort. However, He refuses to do it alone, and He waits for us so perfectly that, if we're not careful, we can easily start to believe that we're doing the work instead of Him. However, any sense that it's our work and not His is purely a matter of perspective and has as much to do with reality as my kids' perception that we each played an equal part in the construction of the fort.

Shadows and Substance

In Matthew 22, Jesus has a question posed to Him. The question, "Which is the greatest commandment in the law", sounds like a somewhat abstract theological question posed by a group of Pharisees who spent too much time parsing such things. However, it was far from it—the question was a much debated one, and had significant practical importance.

The reason was grounded in the religious lens through which they were looking. They believed that, through obedience to the law, they would be able to earn favor with God. Therefore, it made all the sense in the world that they would try to determine which laws were the most important—the weightiest—so that they would at least make sure they obeyed those. Therefore, when they posed this question to Jesus, they were really asking, "What do I have to do to earn favor with God?" Of course, Jesus would have understood not just their question but the intent behind it, which makes His answer all the more fascinating.

Without commenting on the perspective that motivated the question, Jesus answered simply: "You shall love the Lord your God with all your heart and with all your soul and with all your mind. This is the great and first commandment. And a second is like it: You shall love your neighbor as yourself. On these two commandments depend all the Law and the Prophets." (Matthew 22:37-40) By answering so clearly, Jesus cut to the heart of the issue: These commands that He cited, while truly weighty, are not able to be fully accomplished. Which of us, at the end of the day, retires to our bed having fully loved God with all that we have, and ready to move on to the next objective on the list of morality? Even honest Pharisees, who maintain a far higher standard of holiness than any of us could fathom attaining, had to admit that they fall short. Jesus, by citing these commands, effectively undid the system of thought that had motivated their question to start with.

The writer of Hebrews begins the tenth chapter with these words:

"For since the law has but a shadow of the good things to come instead of the true form of these realities, it can never, by the same sacrifices that are continually offered every year, make perfect those who draw near. Otherwise, would they not have ceased to be offered, since the worshipers, having once been cleansed, would no longer have any consciousness of sins?" (Hebrews 10:1-2)

The law is shadow, not substance. It's not that it doesn't mean anything—in fact, its very significance is found in the fact that it points towards that which means *everything*. However, by itself, it is not able to save, and that's Jesus' point in answering the question. Paul says this clearly in Romans 3:20—*"For by works of the law no human being will be justified in his sight, since through the law comes knowledge of sin."* Any honest Pharisee, like any honest person among us, hears Jesus' response to the question and recognizes just how far from holiness each of us are. The law, then, fulfills its purpose by giving each of us knowledge of sin.

However, that's not the lone purpose of the law. Jesus tells us in Matthew 5:18 that "not an iota will pass from the law until it is all accomplished." The law, then, doesn't go away, but it's also not a path to favor with God. Which brings us all the way back to my friend sitting across the lunch table from me, wrestling with the integration of his life and his new found faith in Jesus.

The Transformational Work of Jesus

The problem with adherence to the rules and regulations that my friend had learned during the first two decades of his life was not that the rules weren't good representations of the moral standard to which God calls each of us. While portions of them represented wholly man-made law, a large percentage of what my friend knew to be the "right" way to live fell in line with the heart of God for each one of us. However, by simply conforming his life to these standards, he would be chasing the shadow and missing the substance. In doing so, he would also likely find himself exhausted, frustrated, and no more joyful and hopeful than when he began. He was in the dangerous position that many of us within the 21st century church find ourselves in—with a far greater knowledge of the truth of God than experience with actually experiencing His transformational power. If we think of it within the model of the hourglass, we are trying to jump from the top to the bottom without passing through the center. We meet God in our worship, community, and through the Word, and then go about the work of serving the body and the world around us in our own strength. Soon, if we're not careful, we'll find ourselves exhausted, having missed Jesus Himself in the middle of all of our striving. We've built a fort—or at least some semblance of one—and we're proud of it, even though the walls have no chance of making it through the night. Eternal work, the only work that lasts, is done by Jesus and by Him alone. Our work, apart from that which we do by joining Him in what He's doing, will never last. That's why prayer truly must be our first work.

The Law as a Pathway to Joy

The psalmist David talks longingly about the law of God in ways that might sound strange to us: *"Oh, how I love your law! I meditate on it all day long. How sweet are your words to my taste, sweeter than honey to my mouth."* *(Psalm 119:97, 103)* It doesn't seem as though David viewed the law as a dry standard to which obedience would be exacted!

As we wait on God and allow Him to do His work of transformation in us, we discover that we are being changed. Our desires, our passions, our motivations—all of them—are affected by this new life of Christ growing up within us. It's at that point that our view of the law begins to change. The law was given, as Paul said in Romans 3, to give us knowledge of our sin. It's only through the law that we can see our need for a Savior. However, once the life of Christ starts to grow up in us, we are able to move from seeing the law as an impossible standard and begin seeing it as a pathway to joy.

For example, take the answer that Jesus gave to the Pharisee's question. Loving God with everything that we have and loving our neighbors above ourselves is so incredibly difficult that it can't help but create guilt. However, once we recognize that Jesus has already fulfilled the law completely, we are freed to simply pursue these standards as a pathway to joy. Loving God in my everyday life gives meaning to the mundane, creates passion for things that actually matter, and draws me toward the work of reconciliation that God is both doing Himself and inviting me into. Loving people creates a flow of joy in those to whom I can extend love to as well as within my own heart as I'm able to pass on the love that has been freely given to me. The law, now, far from being simply an impossible standard that I can't live up to, becomes the best possible way to live, purely because I no longer have to live up to it.

That was the great risk that I took in my pastoral counseling that afternoon—a belief that the transformational work of the Holy Spirit actually happens, that new life is generated in us through Jesus and that, as it happens, our lives naturally begin to look more like Jesus Himself. Rather than seeking to conform his life to a set of standards, my friend allowed Jesus to change Him and order his life the way that Jesus desired. The beauty was that, after six months of pursuit of Jesus, the vast majority of the issues were resolved. Addictions broken. Desires changed. Messy situations that were cleaned up, not because he had attacked with legalistic fervor, but because the Holy Spirit had gone before him and made a way.

Of course, it didn't go perfectly. There were, and are, bumps in the road. That's because my friend, just like his pastor, still has a sinful nature. There are times that we both aren't satisfied with the work of prayer and believe that we can do something whether God is working in that area or not. There are other times where we settle for far less than God is offering to us and, in doing so, we slow the work of transformation. And there are still other times where both of us, my friend and I, refuse the work of God in our lives. We hold on to areas, thinking that we know better how to achieve joy. Of course, we're both always wrong, but we can be very stubborn men and can be quite slow learners.

At least his pastor can.

Prayer as the First Work
Questions for Reflection

1. What are some areas where you've tried to conform your life to a standard of obedience, but have fallen short and gotten frustrated?

2. Does prayer seem like work to you? Why or why not?

3. Are there areas of your life where you can see that God is desiring to work, but you're not willing to join Him in that work?

4. Do you think you're more tempted to run ahead of God, or lag behind?

5. How do you see the law of God? Does it give you joy or frustration?

6. Is it difficult for you to answer the question "How do you see Jesus at work in your life and in the world around you?" Why do you think that is?

CHAPTER SIX
Serving the Body

"More than any other single way, the grace of humility is worked into our lives through the discipline of service. Nothing disciplines the inordinate desires of the flesh like service, and nothing transforms the desires of the flesh like serving in hiddenness. The flesh whines against service but screams against hidden service. It strains and pulls for honor and recognition."

- Richard Foster

The large room, though borrowed, was a perfect place for the meal. One by one, the men wandered up the stairs and wandered around the borrowed room, peering out the windows and investigating the doorways and dark corners. The noise from the street below floated through the windows, but it was slowly fading as the hum of blended voices changed to individual conversations with each passing moment. The light outside was fading as well, and the noise and activity of the city was changing along with it.

Inside the room, familiar friends were engaged in easy conversation. While this particular gathering was sacred in many ways, these friends had really become family over the years, and the pockets of animated discussion more closely resembled a large group of brothers coming back together under one roof after a busy day in their various jobs. One by one, as each entered, they were warmly greeted and they quickly entered into the conversation. The room was alive with stories and laughter. The smell of the roasted lamb that was being prepared below gave the gathering an almost festive atmosphere. A few young men moved quickly in and out of the room, bringing in flat pieces of freshly baked bread, along with assorted greens and other portions of the meal that was to come. However, they were largely unnoticed by the group of friends as they appeared and disappeared while they went about their appointed tasks. They had agreed to provide the meal, and they were ably doing so. And of course, the wineskins were stowed safely in the corner of the room, the corner nearest to the low table, ready for the evening meal.

The Master, however, remained a bit apart from the bulk of the conversation. When addressed directly, He easily engaged, but just as quickly, it seemed, He drifted back into His own thoughts. If His behavior was noted at all, it was quickly dismissed—the friends were used to seeing Him deep in thought as He surveyed the situation in which they found themselves. After all, He was the Teacher, and He seemed to notice things that most others missed. That was part of what had fascinated them about Him. If He might have been a little bit more somber that particular evening, that specific detail was lost on them.

The clumps of conversation slowly converged towards the table on the far side of the large room. As the individual groups began to merge into one, the animated conversation began to be punctuated by uneasy glances around the group. They each were seemingly waiting for someone else to recognize the grand omission, but no one wanted to be the one to notice. Each secretly hoped one of the others would step forward—in fact, they each had a name in mind that they felt would be the most appropriate. However, no one did.

The streets of the city were heavily trafficked by a great variety of travelers, from man to beast. Horse-drawn chariots escorted Roman soldiers to various destinations throughout the city. Wealthy businessmen sat atop camels, which walked with a steady gait through the city streets. Vendors led donkeys, piled high with their wares, to and from the various markets. And the people. Hundreds, even thousands, of them, moved to and fro through the narrow city streets, their sandals kicking up dust with each step. A brief walk from one house to another provided a layer of grime that stretched from mid-calf down to the sole of the foot—a full day of walking through the city gave every square inch from knee to foot an unmentionable coating of caked-on filth. Not only that, but these men were gathering for a sacred dinner, a holy rite that had been passed down for generations. It was vital that they approach the table cleansed from the city around them.

The Master moved away from the table, which brought the loud conversations to hushed whispers. Each watched as He moved, wondering how He would handle this moment. Who would be chosen? For the last three years, each of them had anxiously waited for Him to call their name, whether it be to take a cherished walk with Him for a quiet conversation in the night air, or to highlight some action that had gone unnoticed by the others. However, tonight, each hoped another name would be called. This disgusting task, which they each knew had to be done, seemed to be so far below them that they couldn't imagine who could possibly be called upon to do it.

He picked up a towel which the owners of the room had hung to dry on the line stretched across the window. The light outside had now started to fade rapidly, and the candles which had been lit earlier began to illuminate the room. He wrapped the towel around His own waist, and silently moved to the other side of the room. He took a pitcher and poured water into a large basin. He then picked up the basin and began to move across the room. Even then, they waited to see which one of them He would approach, assuming that He had graciously filled the basin and donned the towel in order to lessen the embarrassment for the one who was chosen for this awful task.

Bartholomew was standing at the far side of the table, and as the Master walked toward him, his heart sank. The group was now completely silent as they watched the Master walk, fearing His course might change at any moment. However, they saw Bartholomew as a good choice—while he was extremely likeable, he was in no way remarkable. Someone needed to do this job, and each of them quickly noted in their minds why they possessed some remarkable characteristic and gifting that placed them at least a little bit higher within the ranks than their poor friend. As the Master stood before Bartholomew, He motioned that they sit down. They did, each of them breathing a sigh of relief that they had not been chosen. Bartholomew swallowed hard and stood beside the Master, awaiting the inevitable command.

The moment when his eyes met the eyes of his Master seemed to last an eternity. He waited, knowing what was coming, but somehow unable to move until specifically beckoned. And then, the impossible occurred— Jesus asked him to sit down as well. He spoke the words out loud, both breaking the silence and putting to voice what seemed only moments before to be impossible. Bartholomew sat slowly, much more slowly than his trembling limbs wanted him to, waiting along with the rest to see what would happen next.

The warm water on Bartholomew's feet felt like glory itself. Jesus had slipped off his sandals and was dipping his feet in the bowl, using the towel to clean off the dirt and the grime from the day spent wandering the city. The fresh water, poured out from the accompanying pitcher, felt like a cool, refreshing spring, unexpectedly bringing cleansing. The dirt was gone. The filth of the world had lovingly been removed. And the Master, incredibly, had done it Himself. Each of the disciples watched in amazement, not with more shock than Bartholomew himself.

One by one, Jesus worked His way around the circle. Matthew. James. Phillip. Andrew. In the near silence, each one was cleansed, with Jesus speaking loving words of affirmation and exhortation as He went. Thomas. John. Judas Iscariot. His blank stare turned to a scowl as Jesus bent down before the one who would betray Him only hours later and washed the dirt and grime from his filthy feet. All received it in silence, except for (predictably) Simon Peter, who loudly protested. "You shall never wash my feet." "If I do not wash you, you have no share with me." (John 13:8) Jesus' reply was enough for Peter, and the circle was completed.

> *"Do you understand what I have done to you? You call me Teacher and Lord, and you are right, for so I am. If I then, your Lord and Teacher, have washed your feet, you also ought to wash one another's feet. For I have given you an example, that you also should do just as I have done to you. Truly, truly, I say to you, a servant is not greater than his master, nor is a messenger greater than the one who sent him. If you know these things, blessed are you if you do them."* (John 13:12-17)

The disciples were incredulous. Jesus had just done the unthinkable. What was more, He had called them to do the same. Their minds were racing: What could this possibly mean? However, there was very little time to think about it. The Passover meal was about to begin.

It's Not About Me?

Jesus often taught through parables. "There was a man…" "The Kingdom of God is like…" Stories that taught. However, maybe the most impactful parable of Jesus' ministry was not one that He spoke, but one that He acted out—one that He lived in the midst of His disciples. John 13 records the fascinating story, and it was through washing the feet of the disciples that Jesus taught a powerful lesson. Several times before He had tried to teach the same lesson using words, but they just didn't seem to get it. They continued to argue about which of them was the greatest, and who would sit where in the Kingdom that He was ushering in. But, in an incredible act of servitude, Jesus clearly taught them the difficult lesson: We're called to serve one another.

The so-called "pecking order" is a pretty natural way to look at the world around us. Whether based on position, socioeconomic status, age, sex, or any number of factors, our minds naturally stratify the people around us. Unconsciously, we place ourselves within the order as well—we are more important than some, less so than others. Serving, then, naturally falls along those unspoken lines of importance. The less important "serve" those more important than they are, and there is no expectation that the most important would serve at all. In fact, if they would, the service itself would be humiliating, both to the one serving and to the one being served. It's as though the world operates within an informal caste system that can seemingly never be broken.

Jesus broke it. And He calls all that follow Him to do the same.

A few years ago, while my family and I were travelling out of state, I received an excited text message from a teenaged guy in our church: "DUDE! Did you see the paper? I'm on the front page of the Sports section!" Now Grant was a good athlete, but his best sport was tennis, and this was basketball season. While he was certainly *on* the basketball team, he didn't play all that much, and frankly, I was pretty sure that I even could have beaten him! How could it be that he had made the cover of the Sports section?

It wasn't until a few days later that I was able to get a copy of the paper. Excited for my friend, I quickly flipped to the Sports section, and looked at the photo on the front. It was a fabulous color photo, right in the center of the page, illustrating the cover story from the day. However, the photo was an action shot of the starting point guard for this guy's basketball team taking the ball down the court. I looked closer—was I missing something? Sure enough, as I looked closely at the picture, I saw the blurred background. The point guard was dribbling in front of the bench, and there, on the left side of the picture, blurry and with half of his face cut off, was Grant. Indeed, he had made the front page of the paper. At least by strict definition.

In chapter two we looked at the opening verses of the twelfth chapter of Paul's letter to Roman Christians. He admonished them, based solely and completely on the grace and mercy shown to them, to offer their bodies as living sacrifices before God. Through this act of worship, Paul said, transformation would occur. Later in that same part of Paul's letter, we saw in chapter three, he taught them that their love should be authentic, not hypocritical. Authentic community seemed to go hand in hand with living a life of worship.

In between these two passages, Paul inserts another admonition. In doing so, he breaks down the entire "pecking order" that so much of our interaction is based on. He says this:

> *"For by the grace given to me I say to everyone among you not to think of himself more highly than he ought to think, but to think with sober judgment, each according to the measure of faith that God has assigned." (Romans 12:3)*

He says, simply: It's not about you. This story, the grand drama of redemption that's playing out all around you—it's not your story. You're the guy on the bench, face blurred in the picture. Just like my friend Grant, you may fill a role, but it's not a starring role. And the sooner, Paul says, you can get that in perspective, the better off you'll be.

However, this reality isn't just for me, and it isn't just for you. Paul declares that it's true for "everyone among you!" Jesus alone is receiving star treatment, and the rest of us are just extras. We certainly have a part to play, but within the divine drama of redemption, it's barely a cameo. More like a face-in-the-crowd scene that's on a screen for a few seconds and then gone. This thing that's happening as God does His global work, just as He has been for thousands of years, is far bigger than any of us. We're all just bench players, graced with the privilege of being on the team with the greatest player to ever lace up sneakers.

Of course, that offends our modern sensibilities. The rhetoric of the self-esteem movement would say that we're vitally important and it really *is* all about us. And we certainly must make a distinction between "important" and "deeply loved." We are absolutely loved by God and cherished in His sight. But that still doesn't mean that this is our game and that we're the star. The photographer wasn't trying with all her might to fit Grant into the frame and didn't just happen upon a star point guard in the foreground. He was a part of the team—nothing more, nothing less.

Jesus isn't sharing His star status with anyone.

Belonging to One Another

We are to view our lives with "sober judgment" in recognition of the fact that it's not about us. Having attacked our desire to be the central focal point of heaven and earth, Paul then takes aim at our drive for independence. This is how he says it:

> "For as in one body we have many members, and the members do not all have the same function, so we, though many, are one body in Christ, and individually **members one of another**."
> (Romans 12:4-5, bold mine)

Effectively, Paul declares, we belong to each other. You belong to me and I belong to you. In fact, in another letter, Paul will say that, unless we each fulfill the role for which God has called us, we will be unable to fully grow up into maturity. (Ephesians 4:11-16) The image he uses is one of a body with many parts, each one designed not to operate independently, but in concert with each other. We each are uniquely wired and gifted according to the plan and will of God and exactly as the body of Christ needs us to be, in both its local and global expression.

The implications of this idea are staggering.

First of all, we do not have the right to withhold our gifting and ability from the church, because we would be stealing what doesn't rightfully belong to us. If I am gifted to lead but am unwilling to lead, I steal my gift of leadership. If I am gifted to lead but never bother to find out whether

I'm truly gifted in that way, I steal my gift of leadership. If I am gifted to lead but am too self-conscious, lack the confidence, or am too fearful to lead, I steal my gift of leadership. The same goes for any gift that has been given to an individual in the Body: service, teaching, organization, passion for children, creativity, and so on. Not only is that gift then stolen, but the body is unable to mature fully, as it should, because my gift is missing. Bad stuff.

Secondly, when there are "holes" in the ministry of the church, those are holes in me. And you. We don't get the luxury of complaining that "someone needs to put that ministry together" and then waiting for it to happen. Rather, as a part of the body of Christ, I am called to either (a) fill that hole myself, or (b) help to find and equip a part of the body that is capable of filling that hole. However, there are two options never open to us: loud cheering and challenge from the bleachers as a spectator, or forceful but removed "expert" critique as a referee. Everyone is in this game—no spectators or referees allowed. Of course, that in no way means that criticism is out of bounds—in fact, that's a necessary part of a solid and growing team. However, we can only criticize as a player in the game, giving all that we have for the team's best.

Finally, it means that everyone *must* be a part. Connection to the local body of Christ is not an option to be engaged at my leisure whenever I desire. You and I each have gifts and, when we're not present and engaged, those gifts are missing as well. Of course, living out this truth is incredibly inconvenient. Late Saturday nights make sleeping in on Sunday morning a sometimes overwhelming desire. That third trip across town to the church building this week can be a time-consuming and somewhat expensive endeavor. The needs of those in my community never *ever* happen at times that work well into my schedule. However, I belong to you and you belong to me and, therefore, withdrawal is not an option.

How This Fits

All of this brings us back to the hourglass. Within the environment of worship, community, and the Word, I have an encounter with Jesus. That encounter, represented by the center of the hourglass, generates something in me which is not intended for me alone. As God promised to Abraham and every one of his children since, the blessing that we receive is not simply for us. We are blessed so that we would, in turn, be a blessing to the world around us. (Genesis 12:1-3) Therefore, as I encounter Jesus and find that gifts, passions, desires, and attitudes are being created within me, a portion of those are intended for the body of Christ to which I belong. I serve, then, not because my position, socioeconomic status, age, sex, or vocation determines that I should, but simply because I have been blessed.

For each of us, this truth works itself out in various ways. In my own life, I was wired to do business. I felt very at home within the corporate world of endless cubicles, reading spreadsheets and conceiving deals that would carry the company through the next quarter. I was comfortable in this world, and honestly, quite successful. However, my life had begun a radical process of intersecting with Jesus, passing through the center of the hourglass again and again over a short period of time. As that happened, I found myself with a passion for seeing the lives of those around me transformed. Suddenly, the mind that was wired to develop strategic plans and healthy organizational structures was now consumed by creating a relational environment where teenagers could encounter the life-changing power of the gospel. In my case, that led into vocational ministry, serving teens for several years in a full-time capacity. However, for the vast majority of us, no vocational change is necessary. Instead, the gifts and passions that are created are simply poured out in a strategic way by the hand of God into the body of Christ.

Washing Feet

It's not about us. However, we are gifted and called, belonging to one another and carrying out the ministry of Jesus for which we are each uniquely wired within the local body of Christ. When we serve one another in this way, we are able to grow up into maturity.

One problem: Jesus wasn't really "gifted" to wash feet. Now don't get me wrong—Jesus must have had the most complete set of spiritual gifts ever assembled, being fully God and all. However, with His radical ability to teach, heal, interpret the Scriptures, cast out demons, feed a multitude, and walk on water whenever needed, why did Jesus find Himself on His holy knees, towel in hand, washing feet? Certainly there must have been another disciple that was more fully suited for that work. Or better said, there certainly *must* have been a better way for Jesus to be spending His time. Why did He wash feet?

Try this on for size: *because it needed to be done.* It wasn't that Jesus was gifted, called, passionate, or personality-suited. It wasn't that He had an open schedule, had prayerfully considered it, or that His family was out of town that night. It wasn't that it was His turn in the rotation. He wasn't guilted into it by a voracious staff member with a gift for selling lousy jobs. He simply saw the need, and filled it. And, in so doing, left us—every single one of us—without excuse. If Jesus washed feet, there is no job beneath us, regardless of our place in the mythical pecking order. The God-Man, less than 24 hours before He was condemned to a brutal death on behalf of you and me and the rest of the world, quietly took a bowl and a towel and did the job at which the lowliest of servants cringed. Jesus washed the disciples' feet because He could.

It is extremely appropriate, even Biblical, that we serve the body according to our gifting. God has uniquely made each of us, and generalizing service to point where everyone can and is doing everything is to deny the creativity and design of the Creator. However, sometimes, we each need to *just serve.* We spend a Sunday morning changing diapers, not because we have unique gifting or passion, but because we belong to the young mother that is at her wits' end—and she belongs to us. We clean the bathrooms next week because the bathrooms are dirty and, if no one will clean them, a salary would need to be paid to someone who will clean them, instead of using those funds to spread the Light of Christ into the dark places of our community and around the world. We set-up breakfast, mow the lawn, serve at a funeral luncheon, vacuum the floors, make the LIFE group schedule, bake some cookies, volunteer at the fundraiser, and any other of a vast number of ministry activities. We do these things not because we're uniquely gifted or called, and not because we have no choice. We do them because we serve Jesus, and this is His body.

And He washes feet.

Serving the Body
Questions for Reflection

1. What sticks out to you in the story of Jesus washing the feet of the disciples? How do you think you might have felt if you were one of them?

2. Do you tend to view yourself more highly than you ought (arrogance) or more lowly than you ought (insecurity)? Why do you think that is?

3. Do you have gifts that God has given to you of which you might be guilty of "stealing" from the body of Christ?

4. What are some of the roles that you could see yourself having within the body of Christ? Are you in those roles now? What stops you from serving?

5. As your life intersects with Jesus, what kind of passions and giftings do you see being created?

6. Are there areas where you might be able to jump in and serve just because there's a need? What gets in the way of that kind of service?

CHAPTER SEVEN
Missional Living

"It is a serious thing to live in a society of possible gods and goddesses, to remember that the dullest and most uninteresting person you can talk to may one day be a creature which, if you saw it now, you would be strongly tempted to worship, or else a horror and a corruption such as you now meet, if at all, only in a nightmare. All day long we are, in some degree, helping each other to one or the other of these destinations. There are no ordinary people. It is immortals whom we joke with, work with, marry, snub, and exploit—immortals horrors or everlasting splendors."

- C.S. Lewis

Imagine the situation: a young man whom we'll call "Hank" went to church one Sunday morning. His church is an exciting place to be most weeks, but this week was an especially exciting one, as the pastor highlighted the stories of several missionaries who are giving their lives for the gospel all over the world. Hank heard stories about the desperate desire for the Word of God in the underground Chinese church, the faithfulness of persecuted believers in Central Asia, the supernatural move of God in South American tribes, and the unquenchable joy of believers in West Africa who literally have nothing material to call their own, but gladly cling to Jesus. Several times during the church service, Hank's eyes welled up with tears as he fought back the deep emotion that kept coming in waves.

Following the stories, the pastor gave a clear and simple challenge to the congregation to be a part of the mission of God in the world. It's not an emotional plea—just a straightforward treatment of the Word as it relates to the missional heart of God. Hank's heart had been prepared and, as the Word is spoken, he felt his heart deeply broken for a lost world. As the first note of the closing worship set sounded, Hank found himself immediately moving to the altar to pray. As he arrived, he was quickly surrounded by a group of men who were a part of Hank's community, and they began to pray for him. He recounted to them how he had again and again heard from God that morning, and how he longed to be used to advance the message of the Kingdom on the earth. He also confessed that the next step was uncertain—while he was willing to sell all that he had and move overseas if God called him to, he didn't really have surety that it was the right move. Besides that, he had a wife and three kids at home, and while that still didn't rule out such radical action, it certainly complicated it. Hank worked as a foreman in a large construction company, so while he had some flexibility to be a part of short-term teams on a regular basis, moving overseas in a permanent way would certainly eliminate his source of income.

One by one, the men prayed over Hank. They prayed passionate prayers which seemed to flow from the very heart of God, punctuated by the promises of Scripture. As they prayed, the pastor joined them as well and, a few moments later, Hank's wife squeezed through the group and knelt beside Hank at the altar. Just as quickly as she knelt, she prayed a beautiful prayer of affirmation both of Hank and of what he had heard from the Lord that morning, submitting her own life as well the lives of their kids to Hank's leadership, regardless of the radical nature of that obedience. As the prayer quieted down, Hank himself prayed. He found himself offering his life before God to be used as a part of His mission on the earth. As he prayed, the images from the stories he had seen that morning came flooding back into his mind. However, just as clearly as those images were there, he could sense that now was *not* the time that they were called to go. Rather, he sensed that a time of preparation was next. Hank had never been much of a reader or classroom learner, but at the altar that day, he determined that he would study the Word so that he could be prepared.

He determined that he and his family would live their lives focused on this mission, and they would regularly pray for God to send them as He saw fit. He prayed blessing over his wife and kids, consecrated himself before the Lord, and, as he finally said "Amen," his voice was joined by a chorus of the same from the crowd around him.

Hank stood up to a round of hugs and well wishes, as most of the men drifted away to join their families. A few very close friends, along with Hank's wife and the pastor, remained and they talked quietly but passionately about the need for the gospel to go forth into the world. They also talked about the need for someone familiar with construction to go on the short-term team that would be leaving in about six months, and Hank agreed that it made sense and that he would certainly pray about it. As their conversation finally broke up, Hank and his wife had a clear sense that they had met with God that morning, and that they were about to take the next step on their journey.

As can often happen with young families, the tenderness of the moment was broken by the agonized cry of the six-year old, who couldn't believe that they "haven't left *yet*" and was "so hungry I'm about to *faint!*" With a smile and an acknowledgement that it was such a blessing that these children had never really known real hunger, they piled up in the van and headed out to the Chinese restaurant down the street. The kids ate voraciously, and Hank and his wife had several brief conversations with the waitress as they talked to one another about the events of the morning. They left the restaurant, and Hank's wife needed to swing by the dry cleaner to pick up her dress that had been cleaned after last week's dinner party. Hank loved running into the dry cleaner to pick up clothes—the hustle and bustle of the Middle Eastern family that owned it made the chaos of his three young kids that waited in the van seem much more manageable. After an exchange of pleasantries with the owner and the pick-up, Hank got back in the van and they headed home.

By now it was mid-afternoon on a beautiful spring Sunday, and the middle class neighborhood they lived in was alive with activity. They waved at several family friends as they slowly drove toward their house. As they pulled in the driveway and unloaded the van, there were excited greetings coming from next door. The Brazilian family, which had just moved in a few weeks ago, was in the backyard. They walked toward the van, and their two children, along with Hank's three, immediately ran to the trampoline and clubhouse behind Hank's house. The couples then spent a few minutes talking to one another in the yard between their two properties. This new family had been in the U.S. for almost a decade, but this was the first time they had owned a home. The apartments they had lived in were basically maintenance-free, so they constantly had questions about basic home ownership issues: how often to mow the lawn, managing flower beds and, of course, with summer approaching, the best kind of grill to purchase. The two couples talked and laughed for a few moments before Hank and his wife excused themselves to change out of their church clothes and relax a bit before the work week started up again the next day.

The next morning, Hank left for work a few minutes early, like normal, in order to stop by his favorite coffee shop on the way to the worksite. As he walked in, he noticed that his favorite barista, Kai, was behind the counter. Kai's parents were originally from Cameroon, but her father had moved to the U.S. eight years earlier, and, after saving for several years, Kai and her mother were able to join him just three years ago. Kai had a wonderful smile and Hank loved her lilting accent. They always had great conversations, and on this particular morning, they talked about the lead her mom finally had on a job. Since coming to the U.S., she had struggled to find work but, between Kai's job at the coffee shop and her dad's employment, they were able to make it all work. However, the potential of a job for Kai's mom would provide some much needed margin and relief, and Kai was excited about the prospect of possibly cutting back some hours and going back to school part-time.

The large dark roast poured and paid for, Hank headed out to the truck. He thought about the church service the day before as he sat down in the truck, and wondered how long it would be before God sent him out into the world to be a part of His mission. He checked his glove compartment, found the spare Bible he kept there, and resolved to read a few chapters at lunch.

He wanted to make sure he was prepared when God finally put him in a position to make an impact on the world.

Ministers of Reconciliation

The heart of God is absolutely that we go into all the world and make disciples. He states it clearly as one of His last admonitions to His disciples in Matthew 28 and, following the pouring out of the Holy Spirit at Pentecost, it's been one of the consistent markers of the Christian church. There is a constant need for men and women to make the heavy commitment to learning language and culture, leaving behind family and friends, and taking the gospel into dark places all around the world. Not only has that need not *decreased* in our day, with the ease of travel and the never before seen opportunities to live among cultures and peoples that have historically either been resistant to the gospel or have not effectively heard it, the need may be greater than ever before.

However, a parallel reality is also true—the world is shrinking. Hank's story is not at all an abnormal one. Our world, particularly in the United States, is a vast conglomeration of various cultures, and going across the world has often become as simple as going across the street. Cities mid-sized or larger are home to people from every continent on earth and often to a vast majority of the countries and people groups as well. In this way, every disciple of Christ is called to have a missional heart. Jesus will continue to call some to sacrifice everything and to cross the globe; however, each of us *must* be willing to sacrifice ten minutes and to cross the street.

This was Paul's heart in his second letter[11] to the church at Corinth. He speaks about our own personal redemption and regeneration, and then states, "All this is from God, who through Christ reconciled us to himself and gave us the ministry of reconciliation." (2 Corinthians 5:18) This begs the question: What have we been reconciled to? And to what or whom are we to reconcile others?

These questions takes us all the way back to the beginning. In Genesis 1, we see God at work in the creation of the world. That creation takes on a sort of rhythm: God speaks, something is created, God evaluates it and declares it to be "good." God speaks; light and darkness are separated; "God saw that it was good." God speaks; land and sea are created; "God saw that it was good." And so on. In this rhythm, God creates all that is. Finally, in the pinnacle of His creative prowess, He creates man in His own image. With this, He breaks the cycle—He declares the man He created to be "very good."

However, by Genesis 2, we find the first "not good". "It is not good that man should be alone." (Genesis 2:18) God, existing eternally as one being in three persons, constantly experiences the joy of community, and He longs for this man that He's created in His own image to do the same. And so, in a moment of creative genius, God puts Adam to sleep, pulls a rib from his side, and creates woman. When Adam wakes and sees the handiwork of God, he literally breaks into poetry. I'm not making that up—that's the way it reads: a series of grunts to name the animals; a poetic chorus in response to Eve. God Himself performs the first marriage, and Adam has a companion, a help-mate, and a lover. By the end of Genesis 2, everything is perfect. All of creation is in harmony (the Hebrew term is "shalom," which we'll look at in detail in the next chapter), and God is rightfully over all of it. It couldn't get any better.

---

11 2 Corinthians is at least the second letter that we still have today. Evidence points to the fact that Paul likely wrote at least four letters to the Corinthians, but only two survived and are a part of the Biblical canon.

Of course, the Biblical record reads as though that lasted for about twelve minutes. It could be longer, depending on how you read it, but it wasn't long. Satan shows up in the form of a snake, tempts Eve, she rebels, her no-account husband stands beside her, jaw hanging open while he stares at a giraffe on the other side of the garden and tries to stretch his neck out like that. Before he knows it, he's eating the fruit as well, and all is lost. More specific interpretations abound, but the point is, "shalom" was broken. The harmony which had marked the world from its creation was now lost.

That, then, is what we are being reconciled to, and to which we are seeking to reconcile others. Harmony. Peace. Shalom. And the crazy thing is, our souls can remember it. In Ecclesiastes, Solomon declares that "God has put eternity into man's heart." Almost like a groove that's been worn into each of our souls, there's something in us that longs for that reality.

There was a moment when there was food without gluttony.
There was a moment when there was sex without lust.
There was a moment when there was wine without drunkenness.
And there was a moment when there was God and man, but not religion.

Somewhere deep inside of each of us, we remember this reality. And we're striving for the satisfaction that came along with it. However, we can't seem to get back there. Eternity is in our hearts, but we're constantly seeking to fill that eternal hole with the temporary, and then are shocked to find out that we're still not satisfied.

The Danger of Segmentation

It's only in Jesus that harmony can be restored. This is the great declaration of the gospel, as well as Paul's great declaration in 2 Corinthians 5. Jesus has reconciled us to Himself, and now He's called us into the ministry of reconciliation as well. He says it this way:

> *"In Christ God was reconciling the world to Himself, not counting their trespasses against them, and entrusting to us the message*

of reconciliation. Therefore, we are ambassadors for Christ, God making His appeal through us. We implore you on behalf of Christ, be reconciled to God." (2 Corinthians 5:19-20)

Ambassadors for Christ. Seven days a week. 24 hours a day. Our goal is to see every aspect of our lives, as well as the lives of those around us, reconciled to Jesus.

The problem is segmentation. Our lives are so incredibly segmented that when Jesus crashes into an area of my life, it's only that particular area that's changed! He transforms my Sunday mornings, but not my Friday nights. He transforms the way I read my Bible, but not the way I spend my money. He transforms my relationship with my small group, but not my marriage. Transformation can come to one segment of life and yet have absolutely no effect on the other, which presents a huge problem for any one of us desiring to enter fully into the abundant life that Jesus so clearly promised. We are complete people, not just individual parts. So, when my worship is redeemed but my marriage is trashed, I'm still missing the joy that has been promised. When I'm free from the grip of laziness but still completely bound in the chains of materialism, I live in captivity, not freedom.

Segmentation is also the great killer of mission. This was Hank's issue: With the purest of hearts, he longed to be used by God to take the message of Jesus to the ends of the earth. In fact, his heart was specifically gripped as stories were told of four distinct people groups and of the impact the gospel had on each of them. However, he left that encounter with God and literally, within 24 hours, encountered those *same* people groups. But he missed it. God was graciously giving him the opportunity to impact the world from exactly where he found himself that morning but, because those areas of life didn't fit into his concept of what "mission" was, he didn't engage them.

Mission simply requires that we see people as Jesus does. The barista at the coffee shop is more than simply a coffee dispenser with a smile. She has a soul, and that soul longs for reconciliation whether she's aware of it or not. The dry cleaning manager and his family don't simply provide a service and a diversion. They have souls which long for God. However, there are entire groups of people that we simply look past. People—real humans— that we come into contact with every day, but never truly see.

When I worked at the corporate offices for a large retail chain, there were two ladies who sat at the receptionist desk each day as I walked in and out of the offices. More often than I saw their faces, though, I heard their voices. Every call that came into the office building came first to their desk. They would greet the caller, find out where the call should be directed, and ring through to the appropriate party to find out if they could take the call. I passed these women several times each day and likely had upwards of a hundred brief conversations with them each week. However, it wasn't until years later that it struck me: These women were not simply a conduit for phone calls. They were people. With souls. And I had missed my opportunity to be a minister of reconciliation to them.

The incredible thing is that I don't have to leave my normal, everyday life to engage the mission of God. Paul says it this way: "[God has] determined the times set for them and the exact places where they should live." (Acts 17:26, NIV) This means that wherever you find yourself, God has planned you to be there. For a purpose. Maybe not forever, but for now. Therefore, my neighborhood is part of the mission. My workplace is part of the mission. My friends. My kids' friends. Youth sports. Hobbies. And yes, the coffee I drink. The gym I go to. Every aspect of my normal, everyday life is an opportunity to engage the mission. God has specifically placed me where I am and has wired me like He did in order for me to be His ambassador.

The Model of Jesus

When Jesus walked among us, He was fully here. He didn't simply engage the holy and spiritual things, but all of life. The gospels recount many stories of Jesus engaging the world around Him just as He calls us to do, but maybe no story gives such a complete example of the one told in

John 4. I'll quote the whole story in order for us to feel the impact of Jesus' words and actions:

"Jesus left Judea and departed again for Galilee. And he had to pass through Samaria. So he came to a town of Samaria called Sychar, near the field that Jacob had given to his son Joseph. Jacob's well was there; so Jesus, wearied as he was from his journey, was sitting beside the well. It was about the sixth hour.

A woman from Samaria came to draw water. Jesus said to her, "Give me a drink." (For his disciples had gone away into the city to buy food.) The Samaritan woman said to him, "How is it that you, a Jew, ask for a drink from me, a woman of Samaria?" (For Jews have no dealings with Samaritans.) Jesus answered her, "If you knew the gift of God, and who it is that is saying to you, 'Give me a drink,' you would have asked him, and he would have given you living water." The woman said to him, "Sir, you have nothing to draw water with, and the well is deep. Where do you get that living water? Are you greater than our father Jacob? He gave us the well and drank from it himself, as did his sons and his livestock." Jesus said to her, "Everyone who drinks of this water will be thirsty again, but whoever drinks of the water that I will give him will never be thirsty again. The water that I will give him will become in him a spring of water welling up to eternal life." The woman said to him, "Sir, give me this water, so that I will not be thirsty or have to come here to draw water."

Jesus said to her, "Go, call your husband, and come here." The woman answered him, "I have no husband." Jesus said to her, "You are right in saying, 'I have no husband'; for you have had five husbands, and the one you now have is not your husband. What you have said is true." The woman said to him, "Sir, I perceive that you are a prophet. Our fathers worshiped on this mountain, but you say that in Jerusalem is the place where people ought to worship." Jesus said to her, "Woman, believe me, the hour is coming when neither on this mountain nor in Jerusalem will you worship the Father. You worship what you do not know; we worship what we know, for salvation is from the Jews. But the hour is coming, and is now here, when the true worshipers will worship the Father in spirit and truth, for the Father is seeking such people to worship him. God is spirit, and those who worship him must worship in spirit and truth." The woman said to him, "I know that Messiah is coming (he who is called Christ). When he comes, he will tell us all things." Jesus said to her, "I who speak to you am he."

Just then his disciples came back. They marveled that he was talking with a woman, but no one said, "What do you seek?" or, "Why are you talking with her?" So the woman left her water jar and went away into town and said to the people, "Come, see a man who told me all that I ever did. Can this be the Christ?" They went out of the town and were coming to him." (John 4:3-30)

Jesus provides us with a perfect model for engaging mission as we are going about our daily lives. There are countless principles that can be gained from this powerful account, but here are just a few that are vital for us as we engage the mission of God within the context in which we've been placed.

Jesus engaged along the way. This encounter wasn't premeditated, planned out, or scripted. It wasn't the night that Jesus was scheduled to knock on doors and pass out the Gospel of John. Those things can be a part of our mission strategy, but Jesus shows us that we need to simply engage people along the way.

Jesus was tired, but He did it anyway. Some of the most clear opportunities I've been given have come when my mind and body are just shot. Sadly, I've missed lots of them because I've excused my lack of connection by my exhaustion. However, Paul reminds us that it's in our weakness that His strength is most fully seen—we need to be those who listen to the Spirit whether we're in the mood to or not.

Jesus started the discussion—He didn't wait for her to notice. One of the most ridiculous staples of modern day Christianity has its roots in a quote that's often attributed to St. Francis of Assisi. "Preach the gospel at all times; when necessary, use words." Now, personally I'm a fan of St. Francis, therefore, I hope that this quote is wrongly attributed to him, because it's ridiculous. Jesus is the Word, and He is communicated first and foremost through words. I guarantee you that if you smile and wave at your neighbor every day for ten years, he won't suddenly run up to you and ask how you became such a wonderful person, giving you the chance to share the gospel with him. (Yes, I know this from personal experience.) In the world we live in, which assumes that everyone is basically a good person and we just need to try harder at it, at best you'll make everyone else feel guilty because you're better at being nice than they are. We need to be willing to talk about the person of Jesus in our conversations.

Jesus crossed barriers. We're unable to fully grasp the size of the barriers that Jesus crossed as a first century male Jew in having a conversation with a Samaritan woman. However, her reaction, even as briefly recorded by John, shows her shock. For us, the primary barriers may not be race and sex, although, sadly, those barriers are still often in place. More likely there are barriers of social status, lack of common interest, and whether we like the other person or not. Jesus didn't simply engage those who were like Him but, rather, saw the qualifying factor as whether they were a person with a soul in need of redemption. If we follow that standard, it gives us a pretty large group of people to engage.

Jesus used something that was situationally relevant. Nothing is more basic than water. However, that was the situation Jesus and the Samaritan woman found themselves in, so it was water that provided the metaphor for reconciliation. Jesus used bread, sheep, seeds, vines and fruit—whatever the situation called for, He would gladly use a metaphor. Once we are able to see all of life as connecting back to Him, instead of segmenting redemption as somehow separate from creation, we will be able to do the same.

Jesus was bold but loving. Jesus certainly didn't shrink from saying that sinful behavior was… well… sinful. However, He clearly did it in love, as the Samaritan woman was not put on the defensive nor did she disengage. As we act as ministers of reconciliation, we must be willing to identify where our lives are out of harmony with the way that God has intended our lives to be, and then communicate those things with boldness and love.

Jesus told the whole story. The woman wants to have her burning theological question answered. While He doesn't ignore her question, Jesus also doesn't dwell on the minor issues. He takes her question and, by answering at least a part of it, unfolds the grand drama of redemption to this woman. There are many hot button issues with which we can easily get sidetracked. We need to constantly come back to the question of who Jesus is and why He matters.

Here, There, and Everywhere

So what about poor Hank? It could be that God will take a person like Hank, develop his heart and skills, and then send him across the world. Or, it could be that he'll engage the mission of God right where he is. Either way, one must never be exclusive of the other! If Hank doesn't effectively love people here, his desire and heart for others won't magically develop on the plane ride across the ocean. However, "here" is a place where the gospel is readily available to just about everyone—there is still a great need for the gospel to go where it simply isn't as readily available.

On one hand, we must avoid the error that says mission is something that happens "over there." Every single one of us as Christians must be prepared to be ambassadors for Christ and to engage in the ministry of reconciliation. On the other hand, we must recognize that those who go "over there" make a significant sacrifice to do so. Leaving family and friends, learning language and culture, constantly living in an environment that is often uncertain—these are the prices paid by missionaries in just about every context. Compound that, then, with the very real physical dangers of living and reaching out in places that are resistant to the gospel and where evangelism is considered to be an illegal activity; then it's easy to see the significance of the sacrifice.

Maybe God will indeed develop Hank's heart, give him and his family the tools that they need, and send them to one of the darkest places of the world. And maybe He will do that with you. Or me. We should absolutely be ready; to be unwilling, should He clearly call, is to subvert the very idea of Lordship. However, in the meantime, we're not exempt from the mission. It's vital that we cross the street if we're ever going to cross the world.

Missional Living
Questions for Reflection

1. If you're being honest, are there areas of life that fall outside of the mission of God? Are there times you feel like you're "off duty" as an ambassador of Christ?

2. Do you see every relationship you have, as well as your house, work, etc. as "appointed" by God? Why or why not? What are the implications of that belief?

3. What excuses do you give for not engaging in the mission of God?

4. When you think about the need for the gospel of Jesus to go into the world, do you see that as different as the gospel being spread in the United States? Why or why not?

5. Who is like the Samaritan woman in your life? How can you engage?

CHAPTER EIGHT
Shalom of the City

"It is impossible, Bible in hand, to limit Christ's Church to one's own little community. It is everywhere, in all parts of the world; and whatever its external form, frequently changing, often impure, yet the gifts wherever received increase our riches."

- Abraham Kuyper

There aren't many things in the world that on which we all can agree. Hopefully we can agree that things like disease and hunger are bad. We can likely agree that a child getting the medications that he needs, instead of dying from preventable illness, is good. We should be able to agree that peanut butter is good, along with dark coffee, Thai cuisine, and buffalo wings. It goes without saying that Justin Bieber is bad, and that there is literally no one in the world who knows how he became popular. The general consensus should be that a professional sports team from Cleveland deserves to win a world championship at some point in my lifetime. Most of us recognize that there are certain things that are simply better with sugar and fat, like ice cream, sour cream, whipped cream, and butter. And did I mention Justin Bieber? What's up with that guy? Beyond those things, we tend to disagree pretty quickly. Except about this:

Everyone knows there's something wrong with the world.

That's not simply a belief held by a small percentage of evangelical Christians. The largest section in every book store (sadly, including most "Christian" book stores) is "Self Help." Dr. Phil, Oprah and their cronies all make a living on trying to figure it out. Every magazine cover, from *Cosmo* to *Good Housekeeping*, highlights articles about how to fix something that's broken in your life. And, in case the outward evidence wasn't convincing enough, just talk to anyone who has ever had children.

The fascinating thing about children is that, from a very young age, they clearly display their brokenness. They loudly cry immediately upon entry into the world. If you have two or more boys, chances are very high that you've been peed on by at least one of them at some point in their pre-toddler stages. Regardless of which words you intended to teach your children, "no" and "mine" are always among the first few and always get the highest usage. If there are multiple siblings, you get a constant front row seat to the fallen nature fighting for its life. If you have an only child, you might have to wait until his friend comes over before the craziness begins. Consider this: I don't know how your house works, but my wife and I have *never* resolved our arguments by biting. When we both want to use the laptop, we typically have a civil discussion about it. To this date I don't believe that we've ever handled it by having a full-fledged wrestling match over the computer, complete with hair-pulling, screaming, and clawing. When we don't get our way, the occasions are very few when that was accompanied by yelling at the top of our lungs for the better part of 2 hours, while the other one dutifully ignored the piercing screams and pretended they weren't actually happening. And yet, these behaviors are commonplace among our children. *Who* taught them these things?

The world, regardless of background, philosophical framework, theology, level of education or cultural experience, can agree that we are broken. Something has gone terribly wrong. It's far from a Christian idea.

However, it does have a Christian explanation.

Shalom Broken

In the last chapter, we did a very brief synopsis of Genesis 1 and 2. We said that, by the end of Genesis 2, everything was in harmony. Peace. The Hebrew term is *shalom*. While it's normally translated as "peace" in English, it really means far more than that. The concept of *shalom* includes ideas like harmony, rhythm, flow, benefit… and yes, peace. It's a far reaching concept that had implications for every relationship. By the end of Genesis 2, we see Adam and Eve experiencing *shalom* in at least four distinct ways:

Shalom with self
Shalom with each other
Shalom with creation
Shalom with God

All was well. That is, until the wild story that unfolds at the beginning of Genesis 3. The snake came, tempted Eve with a piece of fruit, she bit (quite literally), and her dumb husband jumped in as well. Suddenly, the world is in shambles. In the midst of such strange details, we can easily miss the overall point. Adam and Eve had been commanded not to eat from only one tree in the garden—the Tree of the Knowledge of Good and Evil. Up until that point, their only knowledge was of good, and they relied solely on God the Father for His loving direction. When Satan, disguised as the snake, tempted them, they were not being tempted with fruit. They were being tempted with *rebellion*. Mutiny. They were about to become rebels and traitors and, in doing so, they would find themselves fighting against God Himself.

When the fateful decision to eat the fruit was enacted, everything broke. The peace they had internally was shattered as they understood evil for the first time and found that it had taken root within them. They were suddenly ashamed to be naked in front of one another, representative of all that they were now trying to hide. Fig leaves were removed from their branches, taken out of the purpose for which they were created, and they suddenly found themselves at odds with creation. And, of course, there was God Himself, the focus of this act of high treason. A relationship that had been marked by peace, joy, and harmony now found the man and woman hiding from God, an exercise in futility in which men and women have been engaging ever since.

Incredibly, even in the midst of their disobedience, they found grace. God graciously clothed them in animal skins, foreshadowing both the sacrificial system and the atonement itself. They were banned from the Garden of Eden in an act of love, lest they eat from the Tree of Life and live forever in their sin. However, God still spoke a curse over them, the declaration that the four-way shalom that they had once experienced was now forever broken.

A History of Disobedience

The Old Testament record effectively consists of one instance of disobedience after another. Adam and Eve's rebellion is followed by Abel's murder at the hands of his brother Cain. Sin followed sin until, by the time of Noah, God was so fed up that He decided to flood the world and kill just about every living thing. This meant certain death, either by having heads smashed on rocks and trees because of being carried along by raging currents, or, if that fate was escaped, death by asphyxiation through drowning, both of which created generations of children's stories that could be joyfully re-told, as well as a wide variety of peaceful nursery decorations. However, God's grace was still evident as He saved Noah and his family even though, before the flood waters could fully recede, Noah proved himself to be a drunk with a propensity for incest. It would be completely inappropriate to re-tell this story if it weren't so Biblical.

By the time we reach Genesis 12, Abraham, the idol-worshipper, is called to leave his homeland and go to a land to which God would lead him. The promise of God over Abraham's life was that He would abundantly bless him and that the blessing would be given *so that he would be a blessing* in the world around him. From that time on, Abraham and his children were very concerned about the *first half* of God's promise, but not overly interested in the second. Many generations passed, and Abraham's children had indeed expanded in number, but they found themselves enslaved. With God's miraculous work through Moses, He led them out of Egypt and into the desert to wander. The wandering was intended to teach them that they could depend on God to provide, but it seemed to mostly teach them to whine and complain. This, of course, made God very angry, so the Exodus/Numbers account reads like a transcript from a home with a single parent with a grumpy teenager who feels like he hasn't had an ounce of contentment in 15 years. In the midst of that time, God gives them the law. More clearly stated, He gives Moses the law while, Aaron, the great high priest of the people, tosses all of their gold jewelry into a fire and watches a golden calf just pop right out. With such obvious miraculous intervention, the people felt as though they were obligated to worship it, which sent Moses into a fit of his own and made him "break the law" in a very literal way.

The law gave the people the standard by which God intended them to live. It included things like care for the widow and orphan, generosity from property owners, lenience on loans, and the Year of Jubilee, which would reset all ownership, slavery and debt every 50 years so that the next generation was always given a clean start. Predictably, the law was followed intermittently, with the exception of the Year of Jubilee of which there is no historical indication that it was ever observed at all. In the midst of all of this, the nation of Israel was growing. At times they depended on and worshiped God but, most of the time, they depended on themselves and their relationships with neighboring countries, and worshiped any thing that they could find.

Shalom had been broken. Between man and God, between man and man. Personally. Environmentally. Everything was out of sync. Even back then, the one thing on which everyone could agree was that *there was something wrong with the world*.

The Promised One

From the very beginning, literally moments after the fruit and the rebellion—at that point when everything broke—God had a plan. Embedded in the curse of the snake after the fall is a promise from God: "I will put enmity between you and the woman, and between your offspring and her offspring; he shall bruise your head, and you shall bruise his heel." (Genesis 3:15) There would be One who would come, and He would restore everything. The people of God clung to this promise throughout the generations and, as time passed, the description narrowed. He would come from Abraham's line. From the tribe of Judah. From the family of Jesse, King David's line. He would be born of a virgin. He would be God; He would be man. And He would save His people from their sin.

Jesus stepped onto the scene and, although the nation of Israel was constantly on the lookout for the Messiah, they missed Him. He was nothing like what the people had expected—He didn't command an army, didn't lead a political rebellion, didn't stand up to the oppressing Romans. He proclaimed His message as though the battle had already been won and, yet, they were still being oppressed. Of course, that was because His battle wasn't against the political oppressor or the unjust economic system. He was battling sin itself—that which had broken *shalom* many, many generations before. If sin could be conquered, *shalom* could be restored, and that was the battle that Jesus intended to fight.

And so, the nation of Israel, the chosen people of God, having rebelled against the law and the prophets, now rebelled against the Messiah as well. Jesus was crucified, bearing our sin and condemnation. In this singular act, Paul tells us, the power of sin was broken once for all. "For our sake He made Him to be sin who knew no sin, so that in Him we might become the righteousness of God." (2 Corinthians 5:21) With the power of sin broken, the chain reaction began. God is now in the process of restoring *all things* to Himself (Colossians 1:20), and He invites you and me into that work.

Bearing Shalom in Exile

But what does that process look like? How do we embody the message of peace and reconciliation in the world around us? Is the gospel message one of salvation alone, or is it truly a message of the Kingdom as well? The clearest answer to that question requires us going back to one of the darkest times in Israel's history, into the book of Jeremiah.

The chosen people of God had been clearly disobedient. However, they were still the chosen people of God. Therefore, when Nebuchadnezzar and the Babylonian army invaded and carried Judah off to captivity, they remained God's people. In a letter to those exiled in Babylon, the prophet Jeremiah gives these instructive words:

> Build houses and live in them; plant gardens and eat their produce. Take wives and have sons and daughters; take wives for your sons, and give your daughters in marriage, that they may bear sons and daughters; multiply there, and do not decrease. But seek the welfare of the city where I have sent you into exile, and pray to the LORD on its behalf, for in its welfare you will find your welfare. (Jeremiah 29:5-7)

These are the words from God to His people, spread out within a foreign land—His words to those who were the message of peace among a people who desperately needed it. In short, they are His words to us today, just as they were to Israel in Jeremiah's day, because we are people both bearing and becoming the message of God in a shattered, broken world. The world around us agrees that things are broken. The question is this: How can they be fixed? How can *shalom* be restored?

Create Culture

One of the startling points in Jeremiah's message was that the Israelites weren't to hole up and protect themselves in the new world in which they found themselves. Common practice among exiles was to move inward, protect, and resist the surrounding culture. Rather, Jeremiah says: Build! Plant! Eat! Settle down! Part of being *shalom* in our communities is not hiding away, simply creating a sub-culture that mirrors the surrounding culture. Rather, we are called to be culture-makers, engaging within our area of gifting in the world around us. The ways this can happen are as diverse as the church itself: Join an area sports team or a bridge club; play music in the local coffeehouse; work with the local PTA; create a community garden. Don't hide in a "Christians only" club. Be a part of the world in which you've been placed.

Do Life

It's refreshing that Jeremiah calls us to simply live. Nothing fancy. Get married. Have kids. Allow the grace of God to increase among you as you yourself increase. *Shalom*, like grace itself, is generative. When an environment of peace and harmony is established, there is a simple ease to life that generates more life, both literally and figuratively. We are not called to be static, silently waiting to see who gets left behind. We are not called to be nervous and fearful that we will somehow get dirty through association with the broken world around us. Rather, we are to be enjoying one another and working to see that joy increase.

Seek the Welfare of the City

Predictably, the word translated "welfare" in the English Standard Version is the Hebrew word *shalom*. Jeremiah's call is for the Israelites to pray for the blessing, the *shalom*, of the empire to which they had been exiled. It must have been shocking to hear God's call through Jeremiah because the Babylonians were a nasty bunch! Wouldn't it make more sense to pray for their downfall? Furthermore, the Israelites' power had been so greatly diminished through the exile that there was no chance of them having any real effect on the political power system. No, they were to seek the *shalom* of the city because, in the peace of the city, they too would find peace. As Babylon thrived, so would they. Babylon should be a better place, simply because the people of God were there. Is that true of our neighborhoods? Our workplaces? Our schools? Our downtown areas?

Barriers and Paths

Bearing *shalom* into the circles within which we move is distinct from missional living (see Chapter 7). The latter bears with it the need to clearly proclaim Jesus; the former is simply a matter of living as people that God has made us to be in the areas that He's called us to live. As such, it's important to see that one is not a replacement for the other but that both must happen simultaneously.

Shalom can be quickly derailed. Anything that rebuilds a barrier, which Jesus, through the gospel, has already torn down, derails it. Here are three common ones.

Barrier 1 - Sin, which re-creates the barrier between me and God

It was through His victory over sin that Jesus initially restored *shalom* and, by our intentionally walking back into it, we re-create the barrier that Jesus has joyfully broken down. Sinful lifestyles immediately lessen our voice in culture, because the message we speak and the lives we live don't blend. However, it's vital that we see sin as larger than morality. Worshiping little idols like entertainment, sports and money, or living conservatively out of fear can cause just as much damage to the *shalom* that we are seeking to bring as immorality.

Barrier 2 - Self-focus, which re-creates the barrier between me and you

When I'm solely focused on myself, I'm unable to take part in the peace and joy of those around me. Time and resources focused on myself (often through the pursuit of comfort and pleasure), have no cultural impact. However, giving away what I have with joy is the counter-cultural way of the Kingdom. Goodness focused on self is simply morality; a good life poured out for the sake of others is the radical way of Jesus.

Barrier 3 - Consumption, which re-creates the barrier between me and creation

Consumption that is out of balance with the rest of the world has its roots in entitlement. I believe that I deserve anything that I want, so I take it.

That kind of attitude not only abuses the world around me, but it very quickly takes that which was intended to be a "means" and makes it an "end." Take the example of food. Consumption says I'll eat what I want, when I want. There's no rhythm to my eating; everyday is a feast day, and food is the central focus. An end in itself. However, food was not given for that purpose—it was given as a conduit for worship! When I move away from consumption, I'm able to recognize the beauty of the combination of flavors that God has granted to me and, consequently, glorify Him through them. Food, like all of the other resources we're given, then become a means to the end of the glory of God.

Just as *shalom* can be derailed, it can just as intentionally be engaged. By being purposeful about the heart of Jesus for the world, we become intentional conduits of the peace and blessing of God. Here are three pathways that can lead us toward *shalom*:

Pathway 1 - A comprehensive gospel built on grace
I'm a conduit of the *shalom* of God in the world around me when I recognize that the gospel is both word *and* deed. If I believe it's one or the other, I quickly get out of balance, and either stop caring for the world around me or stop telling them why I care. The gospel is built on grace, which gives me the ability to speak truth and beauty, not condemnation, and serve with love and compassion, not with pity.

Pathway 2 - Working out of gifting and placement
When we are freed from sin, self-focus and consumption, we can then use what we have for the sake of the world around us. Those who have been blessed with cooking ability cook for the neighborhood. Those who have been given a passion for gardening create beauty, not only in their yards, but in the elderly woman's yard down the street. Those with a knack for building and mechanics use their ability to be a blessing in the world around them, building, creating and repairing. The opportunities are as individual as we are, but the result, in each instance, is the flow of *shalom* into the world.

Pathway 3 - Act in community in the community
We must never forget that God is not simply redeeming individuals—He's redeeming a community. As we live with each other in mind, we pool our giftings, passions and motivations to make an impact on the world. The cook, builder and gardener work together as a blessing in the home for orphaned boys. The musician and the coffee connoisseur work together to create a lovely evening for the recovery house. The woman with great ideas but who can sometimes lack drive pairs with the organized go-getter and, what neither would have done alone, they are able to accomplish a task together.

Do Something
The challenge with the value of bringing *shalom* into the brokenness of the world is that the world is… broken. Where do we start? As the familiar adage goes, you do it like you eat an elephant—one bite at a time. The task can be overwhelming when looked at in the whole. However, if we remain overwhelmed, we quickly get immobilized and do nothing. Sadly, the American church landscape is dotted with those who set out with the most noble desires, but ultimately do nothing because the task is simply too large. We need to do *something*. Get connected to a local non-profit. Serve an elderly person in your neighborhood. Create a gathering point in your backyard for the kids who typically just wander the streets near your house. Set up a free art exhibit and coffee bar on a Saturday afternoon in the rough section of town. Take bagels to work. Refill the paper in the copy machine. Make an effort to have every place where you spend time be better because you're there, and Jesus is within you, and He is restoring all things to Himself.

Shalom.

Shalom of the City
Questions for Reflection

1. What are some examples of the brokenness of the world in the community around you?

2. Do you pray for and seek the *shalom* of the community where you live? In what ways are you more insulated from the community than connected to it?

3. Have you experienced the restoration of *shalom* in all four of the ways talked about in this chapter? In which of these areas do you need to ask God to do some more work?

4. Which of the barriers to *shalom* are you most prone to?

5. Which of the paths to *shalom* resonates the most with you?

6. What's one thing that you can start to do in the next week that can help bring peace to the community where you've been placed?

Conclusion

And so, the journey is complete. We began as a grain of sand at the top of the hourglass, and flowed through, one value at a time. Here's the journey we've been on:

Living as worshipers, we seek to connect every aspect of our life to the reality of Jesus. This means that there is much more than singing hymns and worship songs that constitutes worship. *Every* moment and *every* activity is opportunity to glorify Jesus.

As an authentic community of believers, we seek to live honest lives before one another. The risk that comes with being authentic is balanced by the fact that, unless we are authentic, we can't truly give or receive love.

Our lives and ministry are built on the foundation of the Word. This doesn't mean that we simply collect dry pieces of knowledge but, rather that we sit under the life and teaching of the Word Himself, getting to know Him and His ways.

Prayer is our first work and the only real work in the life of the believer. Transformation comes from an encounter with Jesus, and every encounter generates something in me. This is *His* work, not mine.

Part of what's generated by our encounter with Jesus is poured out in serving the body of Christ. At times, this happens in specific areas of giftedness and passion. At other times, we simply serve because something needs to be done.

We are called to live our lives invested in the mission of God. This can be expressed all around the world, but also must be expressed right where we are at any given time, recognizing that the situations in which we find Ourselves are planned for us by God.

Finally, we are called to bear the *shalom* of Jesus into the cities and communities in which we live and interact. The restorative work of God happens in us, but also should flow out of us in a way that impacts the culture around us as well.

It's important to recognize that these values are not ever intended to be multiple choice. As believers in Jesus, we should be engaging each of these values simultaneously as we grow up in Him. As such, they provide an excellent tool for evaluation: In what areas am I strong? In what areas do I need to grow? Are there areas in which I'm getting stuck? Areas that I'm not visiting at all?

This brings us to the final step. We began our journey at the top, made the transformational trip through the center, and then were poured out on the bottom as a blessing to the body and the world. Just like an hourglass, if it's left alone, the process stops. Instead, the glass needs to be turned over, and the process must start again. One trip through the hourglass doesn't make a disciple—the process must continue, over and over again, until we finally arrive in the presence of Jesus Himself. If we are effective at being poured out, we reach the bottom desperately in need of being refreshed in the top part of the hourglass. If the top portion is effective, worship, community and connection to the Word are never duty, but always joy. They fill us back up again, creating the environment for another encounter with Jesus. Time and time again, the hourglass turns, and we pass through the center, being transformed increasingly into His likeness.

At the outset, we determined that the Family Values would make up the content of this book, and that the hourglass process of discipleship would make up its form. However, content and form mean nothing without participants. Disicples. Co-pilgrims. You. Me. Each of us as individuals, choosing to live and grow together. Following Him.

From one grain of sand to another, it's a joy to be on this journey with you.

Acknowledgements

If I'm being honest, which I might as well be since very few people read this far back in the book anyway, this project was far more difficult than I had anticipated. It turns out that the study guides that I have written in the past have a lot more blank space (and therefore, many fewer words!), which all translates to the fact that I should have started each stage: writing, revising and editing, significantly sooner than I did. However, that said, it's a great joy to be able to put on paper what has been such a labor of love undertaken by all of us as leaders at York Alliance over these past few years. I believe deeply in these values, and have been overjoyed to see each and every one of them embodied again and again within our fellowship.

My first and constant thank You is to my Savior and Lord Jesus. I never thought that I would be teaching and preaching and writing with my life, and now I can't imagine doing anything else. God, Your plans are incredible, and your love is extravagant. Thank You for the gifting to get these words on paper, and the supernatural ability to do it quickly enough to fit into a schedule.

There are so many people that help to make projects like this a reality. I can't thank you all, but I can hopefully mention at least a few. A huge thank you to Linda Horsman for listening to the initial sermon series via podcast and then giving loads of feedback along the way. You're a great encouragement and your insights were always so helpful! Thank you to Elliott Shuey for creating the cover design and layout for the book. You're an incredible designer, and a great friend. The latter is always more valuable than the former, but being able to work together on a project like this, the two make a great combination. Thank you once again to the Elders and the staff who graciously give me the margin and space that I need to write. This one was more consuming than most, and I'm actually looking forward to things getting back to normal. Thanks to Joel Comiskey and his team for believing in this project, giving great feedback, and pushing to make this a reality. Thanks to Nancy, John, and Mike for giving initial feedback as the writing process got started. And a HUGE thank you to Tim Shuey, editor extraordinaire. It's incredible to me that you can do what you do! Thank you for making me sound good time and time again, and thank you for doing all of the last minute work on this one. I'll try to start a little sooner next time.

One of the authors I enjoy reading lists the soundtrack for each of his books—everyone that he listened to as he wrote. In like practice, the soundtrack for this book, available at a record store near you (or more likely, online): Josh Garrels, which was on repeat so often I could almost stop there; Daniel Ellsworth and the Great Lakes; M. Ward and Andrew Bird (who both released new albums just in time for this project—thanks, guys); the brilliant new album from The Followers (if you don't have it, you MUST get it!); Sara Groves; Sandra McCracken; and The Civil Wars. I'm sure when you recorded these albums, part of your motivation was to support my writing. Thanks for thinking of me.

Last, but never least (and always most!), is my family. This book was taxing both from a time and focus perspective. Thank you for persevering with me. To Tia, Ethan, Josiah, and Micah—as soon as I get a few days sleep, I'll be ready to play again! I'm so proud of each of you but, particularly Tia and Ethan, as you've journeyed through this sometimes challenging year. And my incredible wife Amanda… what is there to say? You are an incredible gift from God to me. Thank you for being my best earthly friend, my support, my love and my joy. I'm looking forward to another 40 years or so. I hope you're ready for the ride.

About the Author

Brian Kannel is the Lead Pastor of York Alliance Church, a growing cell church in south central Pennsylvania. He is also the author of numerous study guides, including *Discipleship According to Jesus* and *Up in Smoke: A Study of Ecclesiastes*. Brian and his wife Amanda live in York, PA with their four children.

37532315R00070

Made in the USA
Columbia, SC
30 November 2018